Cotton, Curry and Commerce:

The history of Asian
businesses in Oldham

Team

Writer:	Ed Stacey
Researchers:	Mandeep Samra, Kashif Ashraf
Editors:	Joanne Robson, Roger Ivens
Photographer:	Shurjahan Begum of Jahans Photography
Additional photographs:	Les Howarth of Real Time Images, The Oldham Evening Chronicle and New Image (Public Relations) Ltd
Designer:	Harmeet Sembi. Art.Ideas.Create
Publisher:	Oldham Council

This book is accompanied by a display
To book the display please e-mail **archives@oldham.gov.uk**

ISBN: 978-0-902809-61-1

Publication: 2013

The project has been kindly supported by:

Acknowledgements

When Oldham Local Studies and Archives was approached by the Asian Business Association (ABA) to help in their aim of creating a legacy for their organisation it was instantly clear that here was a project that had the potential to be groundbreaking in a number of ways.

Two years later with the archives of the Asian Business Association fully catalogued and with a book, display and oral history collection within in the public domain the achievements of the Asian Business Association and Asian businesses in Oldham will now act to provide inspiration for the entrepreneurs of the future.

None of this would have been possible without the assistance of the Heritage Lottery Fund who provided financial backing to the project and the availability of the project officers who were able to offer all sorts of help and advice as and when requested.

We would like to thank the members of the ABA for approaching us with their ideas about the project, and in particular Anwar Choudhary who kindly allowed the project archivist full access to the archives of the ABA and who was able to resolve any queries about the collection.

One of the main components of the project was the collection of oral histories from members of the ABA, the Asian business community and other major figures involved in the wider business community. To them we owe a debt of gratitude for their often candid and moving testimony that has provided the backbone of the story of the ABA and Asian businesses in Oldham. In this regard we were kindly assisted by the North West Sound Archive who provided training and advice regarding oral history, and to Mandeep Samra who undertook the interviews with her exceptional professional skill and understanding.

We would also like to thank Kashif Ashraf for his infectious enthusiasm for the heritage of Oldham and for this project in particular. His co-ordinating and negotiating skills in arranging for the interviews and the collection of archives from the participants made the organisation of the project significantly smoother than it could have been.

Accompanying the individual case studies is a series of photographs taken by Shurjahan Begum which brilliantly encapsulate the personas of the contributors. Additional images have been contributed by Tariq Amin, Kashif Ashraf, Anwar Choudhry, John Gracie, Steve Grant, Les Howarth of Realtime Images, the Kumpavat family, Mushukul Hoque, Michael Meacher, New Image, PS Events, Mushtaq Ahmed, Ed Stacey, Akhtar Zahid, The Oldham Chronicle and Oldham Council. We thank all contributors for their kind permission to make use of their images for this publication.

Thanks are also due to Harmeet Sembi for his skill in designing the book and display; and to our volunteers who worked on the project, including Ruth Major for her assistance in cataloguing the archives.

Finally we would like to thank Ed Stacey for writing the book and for access to all his knowledge of the business history of Oldham over the last thirty years, without which the project would have been much the poorer.

This was a project in which all participants were completely engaged and whose enthusiasm was maintained from the beginning to the end.

Roger Ivens, June 2013

The Archives:
The oral histories (Ref: M185) and the archives of the Asian Business Association (Ref: M166) on which this book is based are available to use at Oldham Local Studies and Archives.

Oldham Business Leadership Group

Oldham is a community made in the Industrial Revolution that since then has continuously re-invented itself through business innovation and private enterprise. This heritage is more than a proud history; it is an inheritance that informs and influences the Oldham of today. The mono-industrial lineage from coal, cotton and textile machinery has progressed into a diverse modern manufacturing economy through mill architecture, engineering, textiles, clothing, aircraft and vehicles, transaction automation, food processing and electronics. Since the 1990s a vibrant service sector of distribution, retail, information technology, office services, leisure and entertainment has emerged. The national catalyst for the growth in the last 30 years has been globalisation and digital technology, but perhaps the most significant driver of local economic change has been the emergence of an entrepreneurial and energetic Asian business sector into the Oldham business community. This has been a remarkable period of change and development in the story of Oldham; a story that needs documenting and assessing before memories fade and records are lost.

The oral histories, the display and the publication have captured the individual memories and events from the last half century, which at the time may have seemed incidental but collectively represent landmark steps towards the modern Oldham and which forms a welcome and important part of our local identity.

The Oldham Business Leadership Group is delighted to support the 'Cotton, Curry and Commerce' project.

Dave Benstead
Chair of Oldham Business Leadership Group

Preface

Cotton, Curry and Commerce is the culmination of a two year Heritage Lottery funded project celebrating the contribution made by the Asian Business Association and Asian businesses to the economic life of Oldham. Using material from the Asian Business Association archive and over 20 interviews with members of the Asian business community, the book aims to celebrate the achievements of Asian migrant pioneers of the 1960s and subsequent generations.

This new breed of entrepreneur helped diversify Oldham's economic base by moving into the catering, retail, and professional services; helped create vibrant night-time and digital industry sectors; and produced Oldham's most successful businessman of modern times in frozen food tycoon, Iqbal Ahmed. From the background of a modest family business in Oldham, Iqbal Ahmed, through the success of his Seamark and Ibco companies, formed a £250m business empire and became one of the United Kingdom's richest men. He is also the highest ranked British Bangladeshi to feature on the Sunday Times Rich List.

This is the story of 'Cotton, Curry and Commerce' told through a collection of case studies which record the rise of an energetic and entrepreneurial spirit which has helped to reinvigorate business activity in Oldham. The case studies use the words of migrant pioneers, subsequent generations of Asian entrepreneurs, business leaders and politicians active in Oldham to explore 50 years of change from the 1960s onwards.

Author's Note

In writing 'Cotton, Curry and Commerce' I have quoted extensively from the oral interviews now available at Oldham Local Studies and Archives. Other material is drawn from my research and personal involvement in the affairs of this period. Opinions not expressed in quotation marks are mine. Any factual errors are also of course my responsibility, though I have painstakingly sought to research and verify the statements and facts upon which this book is based.

I have always striven to faithfully capture the exact oral quotation, but on occasions have edited the spoken words for clarity and written grammatical constraints. I earnestly believe that none of these minor alterations result in any change of context, emphasis or factual content.

May I also pay tribute to Mandeep Samra for her skill and professionalism in conducting the interviews and compiling the recordings. I found the oral histories a joy to listen to, and her ability to enable the interviewee to be at ease and talk freely is exceptional.

Finally, a fulsome vote of thanks to my 'gang of three': Kashif Ashraf, Joanne Robson and Roger Ivens. The writing of 'Cotton, Curry and Commerce' has been a labour of love, but a longer and more challenging labour than I would have believed possible when I accepted the assignment. The regular meetings, support and encouragement, help with research and intelligent editing by 'the gang' have been absolutely central to completing the project. Their contributions have resulted in a quality of publication that gives me much pride and satisfaction. I hope the readers of the book, the listeners to the oral histories, and the viewers of the display also find the outcomes of this project enjoyable, enlightening and an accurate record of this remarkable period in Oldham's history.

Ed Stacey, June 2013

Contents

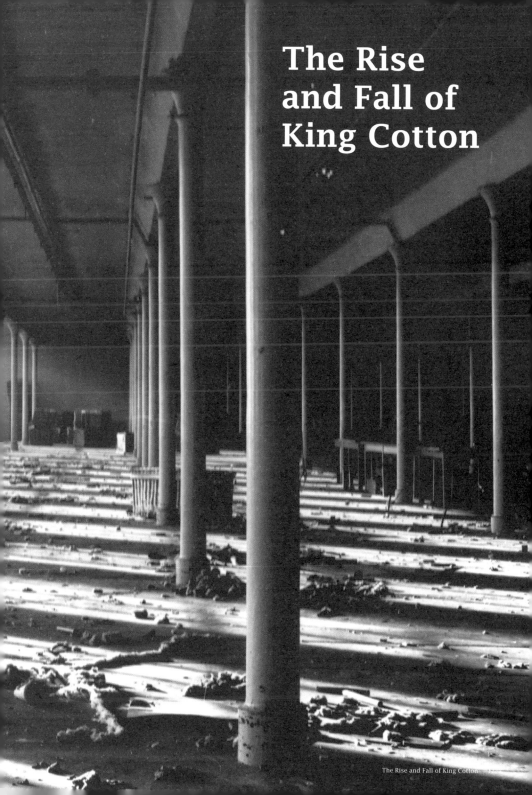

The Rise
and Fall of
King Cotton

The Rise and Fall of King Cotton

If 'Britain's bread hangs by Lancashire's thread', then Oldham's very existence hangs by skeins of cotton. 'Britain's Bread' was a Government inspired slogan widely used in the aftermath of World War Two in a drive to rebuild Britain's war shattered economy. It held true to an extent, for in the 1950s half of the country's foreign income earnings came from the textile industry in the North West of England. But the whole of Oldham's life style at that time can very fairly be said to have depended on King Cotton – the spinning of cotton thread and the manufacture of textile machinery.

Before the 1760s, cloth making was a family based 'cottage' industry using mainly wool and flax. With sheep farming and flax growing a staple land use, spinning and weaving were common place throughout the United Kingdom, with the North West having no special pre-eminence in textile production. A typical weaver's cottage would have had the wife and children of the household spinning enough yarn for the man of the house to weave into cloth on a hand loom. These craft skills had existed for centuries, and the manual methods of spinning and weaving provided sufficient cloth to meet domestic demand. But when the emergence of overseas territories of the British Empire led to the import of raw cotton and an export demand for cloth, the balance of demand and supply was upset paving the way for an industrial revolution which changed the way people worked and lived for ever.

The three drivers of the Industrial Revolution are held to be cloth making, iron smelting and steam power. These three elements combined in Oldham to transform a hilltop Pennine village into the world's centre for both cotton spinning, and the manufacture of textile machinery.

Oldham can claim to have the first water powered cotton mill in the world at Thorp Mill, Royton. It was built in 1764 and was used for carding cotton – the early part of

the spinning process. Within a year a dozen similarly powered carding mills were in use and Oldham's contribution to the Industrial Revolution had begun.

Water powered cotton spinning and milling came to Oldham in 1778 when Lees Hall Mill was built. Within a year 11 other mills had been constructed and by 1818 there were 19. However at this stage Oldham was still not a significant centre for cotton spinning compared to Manchester or Bolton. It took the advent of steam engines and the local availability of easily mined seams of coal to really accelerate the industrialisation of Oldham.

Although cotton dominates Oldham's economic history the importance of local coal mining needs to be recognised as a major influence on the town. The writer Daniel Defoe on a visit to Oldham in 1724 described it as a place of '...Coals...upon the top of the highest hills' with coal seams lying so near to the surface that little, if any, digging was necessary. No

wonder that given the need for coal to power steam engines the steam driven industrial revolution found fertile ground in Oldham. By 1832 Oldham boasted 37 collieries producing about 200,000 tons a year. The world's first steam powered cotton mill was built in Manchester in 1781 and it was 13 years later when Oldham built its first steam powered cotton spinning mill again at Lees Hall Mill.

In 1795 Oldham had 22 cotton mills, and by 1805 the number had risen to 30. By 1825 Edward Baines recorded that over 65 mills existed in Oldham and all but two had been built since 1800. Of the 6,982 families in the parish of Oldham, 6,667 were involved in some way in the cotton industry. By 1833 over 11,000 people worked in mills and the transformation of the Oldham cottage industries to factory production had been virtually completed. Oldham was a first-born child of the Industrial Revolution and one of the world's first boom towns based on an industrial sector. That sector was spinning cotton thread and manufacturing the machinery to do so.

The nineteenth century saw Oldham transformed. During this period Oldham became the most productive cotton-spinning town in the world overtaking the major urban centres of Manchester and Bolton particularly as a result of a mill building boom in the 1860s and 1870s. In 1871 Oldham alone spun more cotton thread than any country in the world except the United States. By 1909 Oldham was spinning more cotton than France and Germany combined. This steam powered textile revolution resulted in a near twelve fold population increase from just over 12,000 in 1801, to 137,000 in 1901. Oldham as a factory town was born.

Oldham reached its 'King Cotton' zenith in the early part of the twentieth century. At its peak there were 337 mills operating night and day and Oldham's townscape was dominated by distinctive rectangular brick-built mills. The post-World War One period was the most prosperous in the area's history with the atmosphere of a 'gold rush'. Post-war shortages and damage to European competition as a result of the War meant huge profits could be made and higher wages could be paid. Cotton workers received a 30% bonus and wage increase in 1919-20 taking earnings to three times those paid just five years earlier. The Chronicle reported in January 1920 that 'no sooner did a man in this neighbourhood get his hands on a bale of cotton than he had his feet in a motor car'. The London Papers nicknamed Shaw – a town on the outskirts of Oldham - 'The Golden City', claiming somewhat erroneously that Shaw had more millionaires per capita than any other town in the world. Life in Oldham could not have been better.

However this prosperity was short lived. Investors did not have the time to build new mills and so were prepared to pay vastly inflated sums for shares in existing companies. Many mills were refloated at valuations of up to five times what they had cost to build before the war and the scramble for shares created an intoxicated and euphoric speculative boom known as 'Oldham Limiteds'. The market conditions that drove the cotton boom were completely temporary. Post-war shortages were quickly met and overseas competition outperformed and undercut the higher cost of spinning cotton in Oldham. This was an unsustainable boom eerily similar to the dot com bubble that crashed the world's stock markets some 80 years later.

Trade began to collapse in 1921 and it slowly began to be obvious that this was not merely a short-term hiccup but a new situation. The world market had changed for ever and not to Oldham's advantage. The large traditional markets of India, China, Mexico and Japan with cheaper worker costs and equipped with textile machinery exported from Platts of Oldham could not only supply their domestic markets but were looking to export as well. The United States investment in the more modern technology of ring spinning (as opposed to Oldham's traditional mule spinning) was another formidable and lower cost competitor.

The 'Oldham Limiteds' that had been floated via large bank borrowings and with huge fixed charges in the days of the 1920 boom were unable to service their debts and tried to call in their share capital. Bad debts of at least £25,000,000 – the present day equivalent of £920,000,000 – were incurred in the ten years to 1930. Bankruptcy, short time working, mass unemployment and widespread poverty dominated the Oldham economy for most of the interwar years.

In a final flourish Elk Mill, the Uk's largest textile factory and the last to be designed for steam power, was built in Royton in 1927[1]. By 1939 about 40% of the 'Oldham Limiteds' had gone into liquidation and less than 200 of Oldham's remaining mills were used by the cotton industry.

However Oldham's growth had not just been built on the spinning of cotton. In the last decade of the 19th century Oldham became the world's largest centre for the manufacture of textile machinery in the world and Platt Brothers became the largest textile machine makers in the world employing over 15,000 people in the 1890s. The Platt family came from Dobcross, a village eight miles from Oldham. They established an engineering business in Derker in the middle of the 19th century before expanding into the Werneth area of Oldham. The Platts were pioneers of cotton-spinning machinery innovating many processes which enabled the mass-production of cotton yarn.

Their massive complex of buildings and internal railways attracted and inspired business visitors from around the world. Henry Ford was a visitor in 1910 when he bought and shipped to the States a steam powered lorry. Sakichi Toyoda, then a Japanese manufacturer of textile machinery, brought his son for a period of work experience in 1921. In 1929 Platt Brothers paid £100,000 for the rights to use automatic loom technology developed by Toyoda. Inspired by the scale of the Werneth manufacturing complex and with the start up capital from the sale of patents, Sakichi's son Kichiro established a car manufacturing business which became Toyota – now the world's largest producer of vehicles.

It was the approach and outbreak of World War Two that brought the end of Oldham's decade of misery and depression. Many men signed up or were conscripted into the armed services. For those who remained there was for the first time in two decades a surplus of employment. Cotton was in demand not just for clothing but for many other war supplies. New industries in munitions, aircraft production and electronics were located in Oldham and the surrounding area as particularly in the early years of the war the region was considered to be beyond the reach of enemy aircraft. Women workers were recruited on a scale never before contemplated to replace men serving in the forces and to boost manufacturing output for the war effort. As a result Oldham did relatively well during the war. There was rationing of food, energy supplies and clothing but hardship as it had existed was greatly reduced.

In the immediate aftermath of World War Two Oldham and King Cotton benefitted from a 'dead cat bounce'[2]. Although the traditional economic base of spinning and textile machinery manufacture was but a shadow of its former self, Oldham still had over 100 active cotton mills. The industrial base of competitors such as Japan had been shattered by the war and the post war world was starved of cotton goods. Now a new constraint had appeared - a shortage of labour.

Oldhamers returning from the war found more attractive and better paid alternatives in the industries that had been set up as part of the war effort and that were now serving domestic markets. In addition school leavers also saw alternatives that offered better career prospects than noisy, old fashioned and low paid cotton spinning. This labour shortage was initially filled by employing

prisoners of war – some of whom opted to remain in Oldham when repatriation was offered - and then by recruiting displaced civilians mainly from Central and Eastern Europe. Over 2,000 former war refugees had settled in Oldham by 1951.

Cotton industry bosses recognised this recruitment of immigrant workers as a successful solution to short term labour shortages – something which undoubtedly influenced their decisions when faced with fresh labour shortages a decade later.

If there were good times immediately following the war they were short lived. The post-war boom for cotton was faltering by 1952 and went into a final and drawn out decline that was to last to the turn of the century. The seeds of the slump were ironically sown in the success of Oldham's export sales of textile machinery. New and used machinery was exported to the emerging industrial regions of the Pacific and India where the equipment could be run at a lower cost by using the machinery for longer hours, paying the labour force less and reducing the number of workers who were required to operate the machinery. These new industries were often protected by high tariff barriers making it more expensive to import UK made textiles. Other countries then developed their own manufacturing industries and made their own improvements, while most British factories continued to use their old looms. A major innovation was ring spinning which had been developed in America at the end of the 19th century. It was faster and more efficient than mule spinning, the mainstay of Oldham and UK manufacturing, but produced a lower quality of thread. Mule spinning had almost disappeared in the USA even before World War Two but in Britain 70% of cotton thread was still produced on spinning mules.

The impact of the two World Wars and the decline of the British Empire gave other countries such as India and Japan the opportunity to build up or expand their own cotton industries. The movement for Indian independence led by Gandhi sought to pressurise Britain by boycotting English cotton goods and using the products of the Indian factories or of hand workers as a substitute.

King Cotton's reign in Oldham lasted for about century and a half. In the first mill building boom in 1841 the number of mills had reached 146, with 15,291 workers employed in the cotton sector. The total number of mills in Oldham peaked at 337 in 1913, with over 36,000 men and nearly 30,000 women and girls employed in cotton spinning and weaving. Post World War Two employment had recovered from a war time reduction to 40,000 workers in 1950 with 100 mills still active in the cotton sector.

By 1960 employment had halved but mill owners still believed that the cotton spinning and textile industries had a future. Although the Cotton Industry Reorganisation Act of 1959 was removing surplus and inefficient spinning capacity, thread spun in Oldham could not compete with cheaper imported cotton. Costs, particularly labour costs, would have to be reduced. There was already a big recruitment problem but this did not just apply to Oldham. The expansion of the British economy in the 1950s and 1960s created substantial shortages of labour particularly in textiles, traditional manufacturing and transport. These sectors continued with working practices such as long hours and shift work which coupled with low pay made the jobs unattractive to British workers. Textiles, traditional manufacturing and transport just could not compete with the better working conditions and pay levels of the modern expanding sectors in electronics, cars and other consumer goods industries.

With the success of recruiting displaced persons to counter post World War Two worker shortages still relatively fresh in employers' memories, the answer seemed to be to bring in workers from abroad. They could take these unpopular jobs at third world wage levels. Consequently 'Great Britain Ltd' responded by looking to remnants of the Empire and the newly independent Commonwealth countries to bring in workers as a temporary solution to what was seen as a short-term problem.

Parts of the globe that had formed Queen Victoria's Empire were 'divvied up' between business sectors for efficient recruitment purposes. Thus the Ministry of Health recruited nurses and domestic workers from the West Indies; London Transport established an office in Barbados; and the Lancashire and Yorkshire textile industries were allocated India, Pakistan and what was later to become Bangladesh.

Oldham focused mainly on rural areas of Pakistan and the Sylhet region, soon to be part of Bangladesh. The view that this was a temporary measure to save the cotton spinning industry was shared by both employers and employees. The Asian migrant workers came as single men with every intention of making money and then returning home to buy land or businesses. However none of these aspirations would be fulfilled. The migrants that came to Oldham mostly ended up settling in the town while the cotton industry eventually died with the last mill closing in 1998.

Pioneer Workers

Early pioneers were attracted by good wages and the prospect of earning enough to establish themselves with a better life back home. The hardship of leaving friends and family behind was tolerated as it was understood to be only a short-term arrangement. These early pioneers were principally single young men who came from a culture that demanded a cast iron respect for elders and the family. It was these family elders who made the decisions and organised the finance that would see these men journey over four thousand miles in the early days of long distance travel. They would have with them no more than £5 worth of currency, little or no English language skills, and no real idea of what life had in store for them.

Raja Mohammed Mushtaq Ahmed

Raja Mohammed Mushtaq Ahmed at the age of 22 was living in Jada village near Jhelum City in the Punjab region of Pakistan. He was married and working as a qualified draughtsman and civil engineer in a laboratory for a French company. He earned 200 rupees a month – less than £20. It was his mother who had heard about the fortunes to be earned in England and who organised from the family's life savings the payment of a 2,500 rupee security bond for permission to travel and 1,818 rupees air fare. This was a big financial decision – 4,318 rupees would have paid for a decent house in the Punjab of 1961. The security money was held for five years and only returned to the family in 1966.

Such was the power of the matriarch that as an obedient son Raja had no option but to leave his wife and obey. After all, he reasoned, it wasn't for ever. The plan was to earn as much as possible and then return home as soon as he had saved a nest-egg big enough to set him up for life.

The airport at Karachi was 900 miles away - a 22 hour steam train journey so packed there was standing-room only. Then he faced the unknown of flights to London Heathrow and Manchester. Five pounds worth of currency - 55 rupees - was all he had been allowed to take out of Pakistan and that had to cover costs incurred during a 4,000 mile journey to England.

He arrived in England on the 18th August 1961 carrying an eiderdown and wearing as many warm clothes as he could. Raja then found his way to a compatriot from Jada living in Whalley Range. Home-town culture and etiquette demanded that he would be taken in regardless of the crowded house conditions. The three bedroom house with outside toilet was home to 21 people who like Raja had arrived in England and whose only option was to stay with someone from their home town. At first it meant sharing a bedroom with five or six people which was only possible with two people sharing a single mattress on the floor and day/night shifts.

Winter Sundays when there was no work were the worst and cinemas showing Indian films were used for warmth and personal space. Bathing was only possible once a week at the local public baths.

His first job was in the card room at Durban Mill, Hollinwood where, for working in the 'dirtiest job in the world' he was paid £3 10s 0d a week. Short-time working meant he was soon laid off but not before he learnt that working on a building site offered better pay. Raja was able to speak enough English to talk his way into a labourer's job on a site in Droylsden and at the end of his first week 'When they put a £5 note into my hand – My God! I couldn't believe it!'

Several building site jobs followed but then this work dried up. At this time Raja was lodging in Ashton and while looking for work he would call in several times a week to the largest cotton mill in the area, the Ashton Brothers mill in Hyde. 'I called there God knows how many times leaving my

address but heard nothing'. Eventually sensing the girls on reception regarded him as a nuisance and being desperate for work he staged a sit-in at the works reception. For half an hour he refused to budge demanding to be allowed to see the works manager. His protest brought him a meeting and next day a letter giving him the job of trainee spinner: 'This is how I started work in textile mills'. After learning his trade as a spinner and switching to night shift work in Stalybridge for one pound extra a week, Raja ended up in June 1963 at Wellington Mill in Greenfield, Saddleworth. The wage on offer here was an incredible £11 10s 0d a week - for working in a woollen spinning mill was better paid than cotton spinning and in better working conditions without the dust and noise.

Moving from rented house to rented house had gradually brought improvement and the luxury of a bedroom that was not shared. By working hard and saving harder, and with the benefit of 4 years of permanent employment and a mortgage, Raja was eventually able to buy a house in Grotton, a couple of miles from his Knoll Spinning employment.

Having his own house meant that Raja had changed his mind about returning to Pakistan and could at last be reunited with his wife and daughter whom he had left in Jada in 1961. What he had hoped would be a temporary separation had lasted for six years. Thus it was in 1967 that the family were reunited in his Grotton home. His daughter had been a newly-born baby when he had left – she was now a seven year-old girl.

Raja settled quickly into his new trade as a wool spinner. Then suddenly after eight months he was summoned into his manager's office. 'What is the matter sir?' Raja feared the worst having had nothing but a succession of temporary jobs over the last two years. But it was promotion not dismissal. A vacancy had arisen for the post of foreman of the winding night-shift department that employed a mixed workforce of Asian and English people. Raja immediately admitted that he knew almost nothing about wool winding but the mill managers were confident he would learn. Besides his language skills would make him the best person to manage the mixed work force.

Thus it was his language skills that helped Raja to progress his career in textiles. Knoll Spinning was one of nine mills in the region owned by the Parkland Group and Raja was in demand to liaise between Asian and English workers in other Parkland mills as far afield as Halifax and Nottingham. Promotion from foreman to management positions followed and his ability to read, write and translate between languages brought him to prominence outside of Knoll Spinning.

In 1969 the Oldham Pakistani Community Council was established reflecting the growth and development of the Asian community in Oldham and its need for representation. Raja was elected the first President. His status in Oldham's growing Pakistani community now meant Raja was in demand to translate and liaise on behalf of non-English speaking immigrants and it was a request for help from the local police which proved to be another landmark change. In July 1970 a murder occurred involving two young Pakistani males - a 'crime of passion'. As President of the community council Raja saw it as his duty to help manage the situation and readily volunteered his interpretation skills. His involvement was such a success that at the end of the trial the police requested that the arrangement with Raja be set up on a formal basis and with a professional fee structure.

The Knoll Spinning management were pleased to agree and for the next 25 years police cars were regularly to be seen at Wellington Mill in Greenfield when Raja was needed to assist as an official interpreter at courts, police stations and tribunals. This individual arrangement became the building block of what was to become the Greater Manchester Police interpreter service.

The structural decline of the UK textile sector led to Raja being made redundant in 1999, one of several rounds of redundancies heralding the end of manufacturing at Knoll Mill in 2001[3].

Raja's career in textiles spanned some 39 years of which 36 were spent with Knoll Spinning making him the longest serving employee of that company. The young man sent to England so that he could return home with a savings nest egg had stayed to make a new life for himself and his family. Three of his four children were born in Oldham and Raja was an integral part of a 50-year culture change for Oldham's economy and people. He was probably among the first Asian pioneers to be promoted from an unskilled labouring job and pointed the way for the emergence of a new generation of permanent settlers who would shape the way Oldham lived and worked over the next half-century.

Akhtar Zahid

Akhtar's father had served in the British Army and was used to being obeyed. Thus it was in 1967 that Akhtar at the age of 20 was sent to England to find a better life. The air fare of 1,500 rupees, which in 1967 represented more than a year's UK earnings, was paid by his family. As this would have to be paid back Akhtar knew he was destined to stay in England, if not for ever, then at least for many years.

'What would have happened if I had stayed behind? We are now a lot better off than if we had stayed in Pakistan. But it wasn't for me to decide. That was my father's decision'.

By the time of his arrival in England Akhtar had received a basic education in Pakistan including five years of English language study but this only provided a very limited understanding of English as it was spoken in Oldham. There was culture shock as well. 'I understood very little. Older English people I couldn't call them John, Jim[4]. Back home, you don't call elders by name; you call them 'uncle' out of respect'.

Akhtar shared a two bedroom house with seven other men, sleeping in shifts and using the public baths. Household expenses were added up and shared on a weekly basis and if someone was out of work their costs were met by those in work. But with unskilled work in plentiful supply unemployment was a matter of a few days, not weeks or months. Cooking was a shared task with much trial and error. Asian spices were available from one local shop and their diet was supplemented with eggs, bread, rice and tinned vegetables, often dented or out of date tins bought as cheaply as possible.

After two years of unskilled work mostly spent on night shifts - at a chrome-plating factory, cotton spinning at Rome Mill, and foam-cutting at Vitafoam in Middleton - Akhtar applied for, and got, a job with Oldham Corporation Transport. Working as a bus conductor or driver the wages were £16 for a 40 hour week but with overtime he could earn as much as £23 a week.

By living frugally he was able to regularly send money back to his family in Pakistan and eventually to buy his first house on Manchester Road, Oldham. As the years passed Akhtar started to save up his annual holidays so that he could return to Pakistan for an arranged marriage.

'The parents wanted to me to come home to get married. It was their job[5]. I would say to them I would come next year but time was passing. I didn't want to leave my buses job so I saved enough annual holidays to go to Pakistan for six weeks'.

It was during this visit in 1976 that Akhtar's life changed direction again. At that time, bus driving in Pakistan was seen as a low status job with drivers as likely to corruptly hire out the bus for private journeys as to drive on a scheduled public service. His father had ambitions beyond bus driving for his son and challenged him to take up a higher skilled trade.

'My uncle said, whenever we want to go on a wedding or trip, we tell him[6] and he brings the bus. I started thinking: when I am working if we miss a bus stop we possibly get sacked! My father then started giving me one of his old lectures: you should learn a trade, become an engineer. It really shook me, that incident, and I decided that when I go back I am going to learn some trade'.

Akhtar returned to Oldham in 1977, driving buses and earning about £100 per week with lots of overtime. He was married with a child when in 1978 he resigned from the buses and spent six months working for free and studying part-time for qualifications to become a car mechanic. Once qualified he took up work as a mechanic with a Manchester motor dealer. But after nine months he spotted an opportunity and left to start his own business.

'In those days people would drive Ford Transits[7] from here to Pakistan. I became a master in converting vans and organising that. Take the engine out, rebuild it all. Fit side doors, windows, seats to a box van, and people would take them to Pakistan to use as mini buses. People would bring me vans from Glasgow and London because there weren't many garages doing this. I was the first in Oldham. We opened a garage in Westwood, Oldham and became busy, busy, working 40 hours at a stretch. I went twice to Germany, once to France,

because someone broke down on the way, and repaired vans on the open road. I worked very hard'.

By the 1990s A & S motors was a thriving car repair business with a second garage in Hollinwood and the A & S Motor Factors car parts supplier on Manchester Road. Today three of his sons run the garages and motor factor shop and his other children, now grown up, work as an accountant, a solicitor, a pharmacist, interpreting and social work. Akhtar is very aware of how far he has come since leaving Pakistan.

Akhtar had been active in supporting the Asian Business Association from its beginning as his business grew. 'There was nobody to help me[8]. I didn't know where to start from. Everything came bit by bit. I had some money but borrowed money[9] from a relative in Pakistan. £2,000, that's what I started with, and paid him back a year later'.

A tragic dispute between an English taxi-driver and an Asian friend in Sholver ended with the death by heart attack of the taxi driver. Consequently Akhtar found himself addressing community meetings to calm tensions and to prevent the incident escalating into violence. This brought home to Akhtar's mind the need for a body to represent Asian businesses.

Thus when an Asian Business Association was suggested, Akhtar supported the proposal from the earliest days and eventually became ABA treasurer. 'I was always interested to have a body of Asian businesses. The ABA gave every kind of support to businesses helping with problems such as parking, health and safety; helped set up businesses and represented interests on bodies such as police boards. It definitely lifted the profile'.

'This country has given us what Pakistan couldn't give. I go to Pakistan very often and I like to do things that will help my community. Here not much is needed when we compare[10]. With the ABA we had the funds and we put them to good causes that were needed in our home town of Oldham. I feel I have two homes: England and Pakistan'.

Pioneer workers

The story of these Pioneer workers – the first to leave Asia to take up poorly paid manual jobs that local workers would not do – is a deeply moving one.

These pioneers would often leave family, friends, their wife and child on the orders of a parent, travelling from Asia on a journey that would take days if not weeks by steam-train and by ship, or by early air travel with multiple refuelling stops. They would then arrive in Oldham to live in hopelessly overcrowded damp and cold slum-housing with outside toilets and find work in mills with machinery the like of which they had never seen before. They would often encounter food unpalatable to Asian taste buds and language barriers precluding any social, cultural or religious life.

Working long hours in desperate conditions for little reward and living a poverty lifestyle in order to be able to send money home and to endure this for years – who would have believed they would see this through? But see it through they did and in so doing paved the way for the first generation settlers.

First Generation

The first generation settlers shared the same motivation as the pioneers – to earn higher wages in Oldham than possible back in Pakistan or Bangladesh. However the passage of a few years and the sacrifices made by the pioneer immigrants changed many aspects of life for the first generation born abroad but raised in Oldham.

Although the journey time from Asia was shorter and less demanding the challenges on arrival were still severe. Typically the first generation had benefitted from education before they had left for Oldham and consequently did not suffer from problems with language. They had a better understanding of what they were coming to - that maybe it was a land of opportunity for them and not just a few years of higher earnings. Better quality housing was available as was Asian food and clothing and the early mosques had established a religious and cultural life that was not available to the pioneers.

However the UK and the town of Oldham were not as welcoming. As the number of Asian families grew, and the ready availability of unskilled work diminished, racial tensions developed. The early pioneers commented on how welcoming, friendly and helpful local white people were in the 1960s. By the 1970s the welcome had worn thin and there was often resentment and displays of hostility toward Asians.

Mohammed Ashraf

Mohammed had been a qualified telephone engineer working in Pakistan before moving to Oldham. However the beginning of his journey is different to many of his compatriots. Whilst most came as single males leaving families behind in Asia, Mohammed came to Oldham in 1968 following his arranged marriage into an Asian family already resident in the town.

He arrived in January 1968 having endured a very long flight. 'The aeroplane had to get fuel every few hours. I was happy with this, thinking I would see all the countries – Dubai, Tehran, Italy. But I couldn't buy anything as I had no money in my pocket!'

As Mohammed had arrived as a married man he could not share accommodation with numerous other men sleeping on a rotation basis as experienced by many of his contemporaries. He had to set up a family home, especially as his first child was on the way. This first home in England was in a rented bedroom and shared kitchen in Cheetham, Manchester near to where his job was.

His early memories of Oldham remain vivid. Snow that he had never seen before; bus drivers in uniform so smartly turned out he mistook them for police or army officers; strange food such as tomato soup in a tin; women working in shops and factories which caused great shyness in a young Muslim male.

'As a Muslim, I was young as well, I hadn't been used to women in work-places, wearing skirts. I was so shy I had to look the other way. I remember going to the Post Office for an aerogram[11] but they were all young ladies working on the counter, and I came out[12] as it seemed wrong to talk to them'.

His work and business career also took a different path to many of his compatriots. He began with a period of unskilled labouring on night-shifts in a factory earning about £18 a week for a 45 hour week. But as his spoken English improved, Mohammed was able to take up skilled work with the General Post Office (GPO) to continue his trade as a telephone engineer. This was daytime work and better paid at about £22 per week. Mohammed was able to study television engineering at evening classes, and after four years he started working for companies in Oldham and Rochdale undertaking TV repair and then video repair. Thus his route into business was not via the grocery shop or food catering path usually travelled by other Asians at this time.

By 1984 with 18 years of electronic engineering experience as an employee, Mohammed decided the time was right to start his own business. The mid-1980s was the era of the Thatcherite enterprise culture and Mohammed was a true example of that time. He leased a unit in the then new development of managed workspace in Derker – the 'Acorn Centre'. With the help of the £40 a week Enterprise Allowance scheme he set up 'Video Direct' to recondition, repair and sell ex-rental or returned TV sets. Marketing was by advertising in the Oldham Chronicle, and Mohammed's was one of the first Asian businesses to serve indigenous white customers as opposed to serving only the Asian community.

One in six of all Enterprise Allowance businesses failed in their first year but Mohammed's 'Video Direct' prospered and grew. He employed people, bought business premises in Westwood, and as the market for TV and video declined, expanded into the fledgling digital and mobile phone market. By 1999 he had disposed of 'Video Direct' and established 'Mobile Direct' as one of the earliest mobile phone suppliers and retailers in the area. In 2005 Mohammed sold 'Mobile Direct' to go into semi-retirement but still retains ownership interests in some property and service businesses.

Mohammed's video and mobile phone businesses were certainly amongst the first 'mainstream' Asian businesses, and 'Mobile Direct' was the first Asian businesses to join the Oldham Chamber of Commerce in 1996.

'It was my son[13] that said we should join the Chamber of Commerce. We went there. They had never had an Asian business apply to be a member before. I was made welcome as the first Asian business member and my brother in law[14] was the second Asian member'.

'We asked to set up our own section but were told we didn't need it and were urged to use the existing Chamber services. But we explained that many Asian businesses would not like to come into the Chamber Offices and speak only English. They understood then and set up an ABA office[15] with an Asian advisor[16]'.

'It was for Asian people who wanted to start a business. They would come to us and we used to give them advice: where to get loans; where to get stock; how to start a business. The ABA helped a lot of people to start their own business; lots of businesses starting and doing very well'.

Abdul Malik

Abdul's father was one of the first generation Asian immigrants into the UK when he arrived in Oldham in 1966. However it would be nine years of working in cotton mills in the North West before Abdul's father was finally able to buy a house in Oldham and reunite his family in Westwood, Oldham. When Abdul arrived aged 12 with his mother in July 1973 there were only five or six Asian families in his neighbourhood. He had only received three years of education in Sylhet due to the disruption caused by the Pakistan/Bangladesh liberation wars.

'I was taken to school to look around and when I started at North Chadderton School there was only one other Asian at the school – and he was on the other site![17] I didn't have a clue what was happening as I didn't understand English – not a single word. The school was very good for they realised that it wasn't only me; there were other Asian people in other schools all struggling with their languages. What they did was to set up an English Learning

Core[18], and there were people from other schools in Oldham. We had a group of people of Bangladeshi, Pakistan and African origins. We had a dedicated teacher to learn the basics and after a year I picked up. It was a really good help having that class. At the beginning I didn't know what was happening, and someone said something about me, and a teacher said *'leave him alone – he is on his own. Don't pick on him'*. I can vividly remember that. So it was quite good, I was never really picked on'.

A further three years in school in Oldham gave him enough English to get by but not enough to go to university. At the age of 16, Abdul started work as an unskilled labourer at Manor Mill. He worked his way up becoming a supervisor and later a foreman but after eight years he decided to move on. 'In my mind I knew I can't go any further. It wasn't challenging enough for me. I needed to look somewhere else. I picked up a trade – building, which I was fascinated with. I joined up with a builder at first part-time. Then after about six months I set up my own building company[19]'.

Abdul started with small contracts for minor work and then progressed to building extensions, houses and eventually moving onto larger projects. Many of these were in Westwood, local to where he lived. The first Indian purpose-built restaurant in Greater Manchester outside of the Rusholme Curry Mile was 'The Millon' built by Abdul's company in Westwood.

With a growing family Abdul had bought the house next door to their original Westwood home in 1978. However in 1996 as a result of Abdul's business success, the family moved to a former mill owner's house in Werneth. This provided ample room for both the growing family and Abdul's expanding community and business interests.

From the early 1990s Abdul had become increasingly involved in community affairs as the Bangladesh community, largely focused in Westwood, developed. In 1995, as a prominent business man and employer in the area, he was asked to become the secretary of the Oldham Bangladeshi Association. In the same year he was asked to chair the Westwood Single Regeneration Budget (SRB) Board – an eleven million pound, publicly funded, five year initiative to revitalise the rundown Westwood area that was hailed as England's most successful SRB area in 1999.

'From my work as secretary of the Bangladeshi Association I had a lot of involvement with the community getting the Millennium Centre built[20]. After achieving all of that, friends in the Labour Party approached me and asked if I would be interested in becoming a councillor'.

Abdul initially declined the invitation wanting to concentrate on his community and business activity. However the invitation to stand remained and in 2010 he was elected as a councillor for the Coldhurst Ward in Oldham. In 2011 he was elected to chair the District Partnership Board for West Oldham.

It was Abdul's business drive that took him from being an unskilled mill worker to being a major influence in Oldham's economic, community and political life. The Asian Business Association was a key part in this process.

'I was a founder member of the ABA. I served on the board for several terms and it was a very good experience: getting involved with other businesses; knowing how they were working. At that time there was a need for it; what to do; how to network. The ABA has helped a lot of businesses; putting them in the right direction; how to set up; how to go about marketing their business. Because of language problems people had the talent but not the English knowledge. So at that time the ABA was a great help. I think now the ABA has done its work. Asian businesses have come a long way. First generation, second generation, we are on the third generation now. I think the third generation, the next generation, are quite capable of joining the main stream, taking on and becoming better at what they do. The ABA got a lot of businesses involved; noticing people with talent, getting them to start their business up'.

Today the Malbro Building Company is run by his sons but Abdul remains as contracts manager. His main involvement is now outside his business interests with the community. 'That is where my time is spent, helping the Mosque[21], looking after the Association[22] and doing my council job. And of course looking after the family!'

Abdul Mannan

Abdul Mannan is a pioneer, perhaps *the* pioneer, of Oldham's thriving restaurant and catering business sector. He opened one of the first Asian food stores in Oldham and then one of the first 'Indian' or more precisely Bangladeshi restaurants in Oldham - the Moti Mahal.

Abdul arrived in Bradford from what was then Pakistan in 1961 aged 21 to join his father who had been working in the woollen textile mills there since 1957. Like his father Abdul worked in the mills and his first wage for a 60-hour week was £7 18s. He shared a four bedroom house with 12 other male workers complete with paraffin lights, coal fires and an outside toilet. As with virtually all his fellow Asian migrants, Abdul had come to Britain with the sole intention of saving enough money to return home and set up a better life. 'Everybody had left their families behind in Bangladesh. The intention was to do some work, earn some money, get some money together. We will then be back home to help establish our own country.

But time was rolling, passing, and after a while we thought we must bring our families here'.

For eight years Abdul worked in the mills, saving money to send back to his family, and by 1963 he had bought his first house which he could only afford by sharing with other workers for a weekly rent of ten shillings (50p) each. Then in 1969 he left the textile industry to open a grocery business, the 'Bengal Food Store', which was at the time one of only two Bangladeshi shops in Bradford. In the early 1970s Abdul became involved in politics as an active member of the Pakistani Peoples Association until the Liberation War of 1971, after which he joined the newly formed Bangladesh Association.

Believing that Oldham would offer better business opportunities for his food store, Abdul came to Oldham in 1974 opening Mannan Brothers on Featherstall Road. He then diversified into restaurants and catering, on each occasion moving to bigger and better equipped premises. The Moti Mahal initially catered for Asian families but the popularity of curry restaurants extended beyond the Asian Community. Abdul invested in bigger and better equipped restaurants - the Light of Bengal on Union Street in Oldham town centre and then the Noor Jahan on Featherstall Road, Westwood. At that time this was the largest restaurant in Oldham seating 98 people. These restaurants, iconic for their time, set the benchmark and direction for the growth of the curry restaurant sector in Oldham. In an echo of the 'Ferranti effect' whereby many of Oldham's electronics entrepreneurs had their roots in a Ferranti apprenticeship, many waiters and chefs employed by Abdul worked part time in his restaurants while studying or saving up to set up their own businesses.

Outside of his catering activity Abdul has played a prominent role in both the business and local communities. He was a founder member of the Oldham Bangladeshi Association in 1978, holding office as Secretary at various times, and then becoming Chair in 1992. He helped to fund and establish Oldham's first mosque in Churchill Street, Glodwick, and provided the same assistance for the construction of the Community Centre – one of the first to be purpose built in the North West when it opened in 1982.

Abdul Mannan has been a central figure in the Oldham restaurant and catering businesses for over 35 years. During this time he has seen huge changes in Oldham and in his community. From the first mosque that opened over 40 years ago there are now nearly 40 mosques in the Oldham area. The growth in car ownership is another significant change. 'When I came to Oldham there were only four or five cars in the whole of the Bangladeshi community and I had one car and a van! Now every household has five cars!'

The business community has also changed out of all recognition. Abdul, as one of the leading businessmen of that time, was a founder member of the Asian Business Association.

'We said we should get together for the betterment of society, the multi-cultural society. We had a very good relationship. If anything happened with the Pakistani, the Bangladeshi, the Indian communities, any argument, any dispute, anything would be resolved amicably. It was a big help to the local economy, earning money, employing people, paying taxes'.

Mohammed Rahiem

Although he was born in Bradford in 1970 where his father was working in local textile mills, Mohammed spent his early years in the Mirpur district of Kashmir. Thus when the seven-year old Mohammed returned to the UK in 1977 to Oldham where his father had settled, he found life to be very different from the small rural village he had grown up in. The weather was cold, his mother had remained behind in Kashmir, and although he had his brother for companionship - older by one year – it was strange to be looked after by his father. But on the positive side he liked school as the teachers were so much nicer and his father's house was big with comfortable bedrooms. Mohammed's father had by this time settled in Oldham and with the help of family loans had managed to buy a large former mill owner's house on Park Road for £5,000.

'My mum wasn't here. I had my older brother who was very supportive. We had two lodgers in the house and when dad had gone to work they would look after us. It was very puzzling at first. The kind of life we were used to in Pakistan was a farm life. A city life was strange'.

'I went to Glodwick Infants. I felt very comfortable there because the teachers were really nice compared to my teachers in Pakistan. They used to whip you proper! That was an advantage'.

His secondary school was Hathershaw Comprehensive and for the first time Mohammed came across racial tensions. 'A bus took the girls to school from Waterloo Street and the girls would pay a fiver a week each for travel. The boys, we would all walk together, meet up near my house at Alexandra Park. The reason for that was there were a lot of skinheads, punk rockers. The Asian lads did feel threatened. There was a certain amount of racism then. It was a case of if we walk together no one would harm us'.

Mohammed's mother came to live in Oldham once Mohammed had started at Alexandra Park Junior School bringing another brother and two sisters with her. Although the family was re-united it was at this time that his father became ill forcing him to give up his work in the textiles mills.

His mother worked long hours as a 'home worker' producing garments on an industrial sewing machine and Mohammed's eldest sister was effectively a second mother helping run the house and bring up the children. 'My mum was the only breadwinner in the family. Dad was ill and back in Pakistan. I use to 'wag it[23]' from school. I would do one or two days during the week[24]'.

Mohammed left school as soon as he was 16 and started working full-time in the clothes shop during the day and also working in a clothing warehouse at night. Two years into the job an older worker at the shop told him bluntly that unless he was prepared to work like this for the rest of his life on a low wage, he should look for better employment if he was to raise his own family. Mohammed had married at 17 and his first child was on the way, so this advice struck a chord. He was fluent in both English and Urdu and it was this skill that enabled him to leave retail work. He applied for and got, a post as a bi-lingual classroom assistant, and later began work as a youth worker in the evenings while at the same time developing himself further through attending various different educational establishments on a part-time basis. His hard work and ability won him promotion to Community Development Officer at a Single Regeneration Project. He then moved on to OMBC Sports Development Unit and became the Regional Sports Manager for Sporting Equals[25].

Mohammed now seemed established in the early stages of a successful public sector career when his brother urged him to join him part-time to help with a new security business: Pride Security. The business prospered and Mohammed made it his full time work. His brother, recognising Mohammed's business ability, stepped aside enabling Mohammed to take over the running of the business. Pride Security developed a strong niche position in the security field specialising in providing marshalling staff for festivals, events and melas. They chose not to provide doorstaff and bouncer security at night clubs and licensed premises because of their faith opposition to alcohol. This proved to be an inspired business decision.

'One area we did not go into was the door industry, the night club industry. This was because of the influence of alcohol in the money we would be paid. From a religious perspective we did not want that. We provided security guards[26] and then started working in events, carnivals, melas. Because of the competition in this sector we wanted to be a 'one stop shop'. If you needed an artist, any equipment from stages to a PA system, barriers, plus man power for event security. The static manned side is mainly in the North West but events can be anywhere from Scotland to London, from car parking to stage management. We then started close-protection bodyguard work for celebrities

such as: Amir Khan[27], General Musharraf[28], Imran Khan[29], Mike Tyson[30], John Barnes[31], Ronnie O'Sullivan[32] and a host of other international celebrities from abroad'.

To reflect the widening activities of the business the company was re-branded as PS Events Management Ltd in 2011. At times they now employ, with seasonal and temporary workers over 200 people from the office headquarters in Derker, Oldham. The company has a strong emphasis on social responsibility, with a recruitment policy to bring people into employment and divert them away from anti-social activities. It also works on a voluntary basis to provide traffic management and crowd security at religious events and major funerals.

In 2005 Mohammed joined the Asian Business Association and in 2009 became only the second person to be elected Chair, succeeding Tariq Amin who had been Chair since the formation of the ABA in 1998.

'We[33] were a support to businesses and those businesses have flourished. Entrepreneurs got established and then were able to go into other fields. Corner shops and restaurants were established years back. Now Asian businesses are in many sectors of which security is just one. Twenty years ago you didn't hear of an Asian-owned security business'.

Ramsingh and Gunvant Kumpavat

Ramsingh was 27 years of age when he left Gujarat in India for Oldham. His flight was delayed by foggy weather with the result that he missed his London to Manchester connection and was left stranded in London with virtually no words of English and only £1 10s remaining of the £3 he had left India with. When he eventually arrived in Manchester things were no better. It was December 1965 and the cold, snow and darkness made this a miserable time. He found work in Old Trafford at Richard Haworth's textile company, and then at ICI's Orb Mill wallpaper factory as an assistant printer starting at £9 for a 40-hour week.

'It was a hard life in the beginning. I had £1.50 in my pocket when I arrived in Manchester. I had to work, and work hard. Then there were about seven Indian families in Oldham but there was no Indian grocery store and Indian food was difficult to get. Once a fortnight a van from Preston would come to Oldham selling Indian groceries and vegetables'.

It was an equally unpromising welcome for seven year old Gunvant when he arrived in 1968 unable to speak a word of English, together with his mother and younger brother. 'I didn't like it at all! Dark; bleak; damp. Coming from a nice sunny warm country, arriving in November[34], it was absolutely freezing!'

'He[35] was working all the hours God sent trying to cover the bills and trying to buy a house for us. When we initially arrived we were living in a two-up/two-down accommodation shared by two families. There was a bit of squalor, but that's how it was'.

By 1970 Ramsingh had bought his first house for £450 in Werneth. As well as working the night shift from 10.00pm to 6.00am at Orb Mill he bought off-cuts of material from Trendsetter Home Furnishings in nearby Brook Mill, Hollins. He then employed home-workers to make quilts and curtains that he would sell door to door throughout the North West.

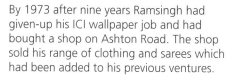

By 1973 after nine years Ramsingh had given-up his ICI wallpaper job and had bought a shop on Ashton Road. The shop sold his range of clothing and sarees which had been added to his previous ventures.

'My mother worked at Park Cake Bakeries for the first five years. Both parents were constantly working and I was left to look after my younger brother. When I look back I felt I was always working. My father set up business working from home and he would go selling house-to-house in towns like Bolton, Bury, Blackburn, Leeds; wherever there was a large Asian community. People would come to the home to buy sarees and at the age of eight or nine I was selling sarees at the house!'

This early involvement in the family business directly shaped Gunvant's career. 'I was an average sort of student and I would have liked to have studied law. But circumstances dictate a lot of things. Business was starting to pick up; my parents were struggling on their own. I wanted to go to university and study law but decided against that and joined the family business at the age of eighteen'.

The Kumpavat retail business grew in parallel with the growth of the Asian community and its retail sophistication. In 1978 a second shop opened selling electrical goods and gift-ware and then in 1982 a third shop was opened as a travel agency, as a direct response to customer demand.

'My father started one business; started another; developed a third. Each was complementary as the Asian Community built up. There were a lot of students[36] from the Asian sub-continent and they would buy goods to take back. They used to tell him: Mr Kumpavat – you do everything else. Why don't you do the air line tickets as well? So he started doing travel.'

By the early 1990s both shops were doing well and were the main business drivers with the travel agency a useful subsidiary. But all this changed when a health scare for Ramsingh meant he had to relinquish control of the business and Gunvant had to take over. It was Gunvant's decision to develop the travel part of the business and by 1995 the other shops had been closed down. Mina Travel[37] had become a major independent travel operator employing most of the Kumpavat family together with other employees.

'My father had a minor heart attack, and I was thrown into the deep end managing all three businesses. I learnt the ropes of the travel side, and one of the things I found was that it was much better than the other two businesses we had. With travel you are not tying up money in stock. There was no credit or goods being returned which was what we suffered from in the other two businesses. Fashion would change and you would end up with dead stock you couldn't sell. With electrical goods you would get faulty electrical goods returned and complaints. When father got well he started looking after the shops and I started looking after travel. It took off in leaps and bounds, and four or five years later we took the active decision to shut the other two businesses and concentrate on travel'.

Outside of the businesses both father and son have been closely involved with the Oldham communities. Ramsingh was a founder member of the Oldham Indian Association, serving a term of office as President. Now retired from business he still remains extremely active in the Association. 'I am retired, but I have worked hard for the community. I am a

founder member of the Oldham Indian Association from 1968 where I have been President and Vice president. I am a trustee of the Radna Krishna temple in Oldham and a founder member of the Hindu Council of the North'.

Gunvant was one of the earliest Asian members of the Oldham Chamber of Commerce and was a founder member of the Asian Business Association in 1998. He remained on the board throughout its existence and served as Chair at different times.

'I was a member of Oldham Chamber of Commerce and it was the Chamber that initiated the ABA. Some 25% of Oldham businesses were members of the Chamber but only about 3% of Asian businesses were. The ABA was initially part of Oldham Chamber. Then as things changed in the Chamber it became a break away organisation. When we had the riots in Oldham[38] the ABA came to the forefront, trying to re-unite communities, helping Asian businesses to build up. We took on a full time worker – Mr Anwar Choudhary – and progressed from there'.

'As time progressed a lot of Asian businesses became firmly established. Even the Chamber who set us up disappeared. We[39] felt there wasn't a further need for our services. We had fulfilled that need and things were progressing fine without us'.

First Generation

The first generation left their unskilled low-wage employment to establish family businesses in the sectors stereotypically seen as the entry areas for immigrant businesses: restaurants and clothing. However stereotypes often cloud the true picture and the Asian business base in Oldham has always been much broader and more diverse than traditionally believed. In Oldham, early business successes were also achieved in building, security, event management, electrical goods, mobile phones and travel.

Oldham's Asian community also was growing in strength and confidence. Out of the first modest mosques located in converted houses a variety of larger mosques, Hindu temples and community centres now began to appear. Representative organisations were formed such as the Oldham Pakistani Community Council, the Oldham Indian Association, and the Oldham Bangladeshi Association. Restaurants moved up the food chain from cheap and cheerful flock wallpapered building conversions to purpose-built high quality establishments offering extensive menus of Indian cuisine, not just curry and rice.

Second Generation

The 1980s saw yet another period of change for both Asian businesses and Oldham's Asian community. The second generation of businessmen – they were still all men at this stage - were typically well-educated and with a perspective and vision far beyond that of the early pioneers. The diversity and strength of the Asian business sector was beginning to be recognised by the wider business and political establishments. Sophisticated businesses were now trading nationally and internationally; manufacturing and wholesale businesses had developed complex supply chains; and there was a fast developing support network of professional services.

Within Oldham the Asian community was no longer a tiny minority and now represented a visibly significant proportion of the population concentrated in distinct areas of the town. Nationally this was a gloomy and depressed time for the UK economy with mass unemployment, workplace strikes and rampant inflation. This economic turmoil was exacerbated in Oldham by the terminal and structural decline of the textile industry and heavy manufacturing.

As the visibility of Oldham's Asian community increased it became the focus of increasing resentment from white working class residents. Segregation in housing and schools grew unchecked allowing racial tensions to ferment that would ultimately come to a head in the Oldham riots of 2001.

Arshad Mahmood

Arshad Mahmood was one of the original founder members of the Asian Business Association and one of the first Asian entrepreneurs to establish a business in the professional sector. He was 25 and an Economics and English graduate when he left the Punjab area of Pakistan in 1985 and came via Heathrow Airport to Oldham for an arranged marriage.

After living with his in-laws for a few months he bought a house with his new wife in Coppice, Oldham, where he still lives with his family. His early experiences in Oldham, though challenging, contrast sharply with the harsh difficulties faced by the Asian pioneers that arrived in the 1960s. By the year of his arrival the Asian community was firmly established with a network of families, mosques and community centres.

'Pakistan was a third world country, so I was excited - the modern airport; all the lighting. But it was cold in November. I wasn't used to walking on snow. The houses were quite different. The houses were small without any gardens. Back in Pakistan houses maybe small but had quite big gardens. Food wasn't that different; families could cook the same food here as there.'

He initially found work as a salesman in a Manchester warehouse for two years while studying for accountancy qualifications at evening classes. He then worked for accountancy firms in Manchester for seven years. This involved spending time on client premises when he was often asked to help recruit labour from Oldham to work in Manchester.

'Manufacturing was quite high in Manchester. Newcomers could easily get jobs in knitting factories, in manufacturing. I worked in Piccadilly and Ancoats for large firms where I used to do their books. Usually they would ask me: we need workers. Could I find them some from Oldham? Now there are no jobs, and if someone wants to come from abroad - India, Pakistan, Bangladesh – it is hard for them. They can't buy a house, can't afford rent and they can't get jobs'.

Though most of Arshad's work contacts were in Manchester he began to get requests from Oldham businesses for help with accounting and tax returns. In 1994 he decided to leave his employment in Manchester and start his own accountancy practice in Oldham.

'I thought it would be hard at first as most of my contacts were in Manchester not Oldham. I thought I will try to survive for one year but in the first month I got a good response. There wasn't another Asian accountant in Oldham then. I got clients from Manchester and Ashton as well as Oldham. Some were small businesses, like taxi drivers, and some bigger manufacturers as well. All of my clients then were from the Asian Community. That is still largely true today as I have very few English clients'.

As one of the first Oldham Asian business professionals Arshad was in demand. He was a school governor at two local schools and treasurer for both the Oldham Racial Equality Council and, for 17 years, the Coppice Community Centre. He was a natural choice to be the first treasurer of the Asian Business Association.

'I started my business in 1994 and after a couple of years this project came up from the Chamber. They wanted to help form the ABA. I'm involved from day one. I remember the first meeting in the Chamber offices. The Chamber arranged events and meetings and the ABA gave me a chance to speak so I got benefit from the ABA. I got more publicity and I got more clients! We had a quite successful dinner for a good few years. There was networking, providing information to new businesses. We covered business topics such as health and safety. The annual dinner attracted 400-500 people at £30 a ticket. People were happy to pay. In the first few years the ABA was doing very well. The banks were keen to support the ABA and the businesses were doing well. I feel sad it is winding down now. I think there is still a need for an ABA'.

Tariq
Amin

Tariq's father, Mohammad Amin, had travelled to England from Karachi, Pakistan in 1958 to support his younger brother who had already come to the UK to study. Mohammad initially worked in the Midlands at Fort Dunlop and at an iron foundry. Tariq arrived aged 10 in 1962 with his mother and three sisters in order to be reunited with his father who had moved to Rochdale and then Oldham and was working in the cotton mills.

Having been reunited with his family Mohammad now had the resources to start a business. The increasing number of Asians settling in Oldham provided an opportunity to sell Asian food and spices and so Mohammad opened a general grocery and halal meat shop on the corner of Huddersfield Road and Shaw road. It was from this shop that Amin Poultry originated.

With Mohammad working twelve hour shifts in cotton mills earning around £1 an hour Tariq and his mother had to be the main shop workers. 'It was a culture shock. It was unheard of for an Asian woman to be working in a shop and serving people. But they had children and a family to raise so they did what ever they did to support the family'.

In 1960s Britain halal food was not available so Mohammad and Tariq would purchase spent former laying hens from farms in the area and then slaughter and prepare poultry to halal standards at the shop. But in 1967 the shop had to close when Tariq's father returned to Pakistan for the wedding of his eldest daughter. On his return bigger and better premises were taken in Barker Street near Oldham town centre.

Though still a grocery store the processing and sale of halal poultry was becoming the main activity of the business. On becoming 18 Tariq briefly considered joining the Pakistan Airforce and going to university before he finally decided to join his father in building Amin Poultry into a major business.

'We started doing poultry wholesale rather than retail to the shops. We started slaughtering poultry initially at local farms and then at slaughterhouses to supply to different shops and restaurants. The circle of supply became larger and larger - to Manchester, to Bradford. By 1973 Amin Poultry was born in the true sense. It was a name synonymous with poultry in the North West and maybe in the whole of Britain. We were known as the 'King of Halal Poultry''.

Mohammad died in 1980 while on holiday in Pakistan but by then Amin Poultry was a multi-million pound business processing 50,000 birds a week[40] to halal standards for local shops as well as the catering industry and sourcing poultry from Holland as well as throughout the UK. A number of abattoirs in the UK, advised by Tariq, were now operating to full halal compliance which was a major breakthrough in the British poultry industry. New premises were established in Featherstall Road, Westwood. Today, Amin Poultry has downsized to allow the family to enjoy a more balanced life-style but remains a major regional supplier to the catering sector and supermarkets.

Tariq has strong and vivid memories of arriving in Oldham as an excited ten year old following a stop-over in the mid-day heat of Kuwait and then landing at Heathrow. 'All you could see were lights everywhere from the windows of the plane and then the long journey by road to Oldham. In Oldham the sky line was full of chimneys. As soon as you raised your head all you could see were chimneys with smoke bellowing out of them. The weather was certainly a lot more colder, I do remember that. There were gas lights; trams were running; cobbled streets with tram lines running through'.

The Amin family was one of the first families to settle in Oldham as the majority of Asian workers in the 1960s were single men. Social life was limited. As a teenager Tariq often visited an Asian café in Huddersfield Road – the forerunner of Indian restaurants that would be so successful in the following decades.

In addition to the grocery store and incipient poultry business, Mohammad, with help from a teenage Tariq, hired Indian language films for screening at cinemas in Oldham such as the Continental, the Empire and the Kings Cinema. These showings proved immensely successful until video rental brought to an end regular cinema going.

'It was a weekly event, on a Sunday. There used to be a massive queue of workers waiting to go in and have some sort of a cultural get-together. I used to take the tickets and be the usher person showing them to their seats. Tickets would be pennies; six old pence or so'.

By 1996 Tariq Amin was a leading member of Oldham's business community and was an obvious person to join the board of the Oldham Chamber of Commerce. The Chamber was at the height of its powers at this time. With a ten million pound turnover and a hundred staff it was working with about a quarter of local businesses but making little impact amongst the growing Asian business sector. Tariq, the first Asian director on the Chamber Board, was central to the growth and setting up of the Asian Business Association. He was the obvious choice to chair the ABA when it was formed. He remained chair until in 2009 when he was elected Honourary President of the ABA for life – a post created specifically to recognise his contribution to the business community. He also went on to join the boards of the Greater Manchester Chamber of Commerce and the North West Development Agency, and was invited onto the Board of the Blair Government's newly-formed Asian Business Forum advisory panel.

Besides his business interests Tariq Amin is also active in education working as a school governor, mentoring young entrepreneurs, and has worked with Councillor Kay Knox in Oldham education. His charitable activities include fund-raising for the Royal Oldham Hospital scanner appeal, Dr Kershaw's Hospice, the Heart Foundation; the Lung Foundation; and in response to natural disasters around the world.

'The Chamber of Commerce weren't getting Asian businesses walking through the door. There was a language barrier. The need, the mentality and the thinking of the Asian business style was unique. The culture difference was the major factor. The ABA was then formed parallel to the Chamber of Commerce. It was the missing link between the Chamber and Asian businesses'.

'For 14 or 15 years the ABA was a very important part of the Oldham economy providing about 18% of local GDP. It's a mammoth amount of money. The ABA helped so many businesses to grow through links with the Chamber, the North West Development Agency; links with all forms of sectors - the bankers, estate agents, the local development agency. We helped hundreds of small businesses and 15 to 20 large scale businesses.'

Bharat
Sisodia

Bharat's family enjoyed an agreeable life in Gujarat, India where they lived in a large house with servants. His father, Jagatsingh Sisodia, held a secure high-ranking position as a magistrate in the Indian Judiciary Service. However in 1963 in his late 40s Jagatsingh gave up this comfortable life-style to move to Oldham where he took up a job working in the textile industry at Lily Mill. His motivation was not higher earnings but the chance of a better education for his four children.

Jagatsingh saw the Oldham of 1963 in a very positive light. 'He[41] realised that Indian Ministers were sending their children for education to England where education was brilliant. That is the main reason why he decided to settle here. In those days telephones were not good communications. The correspondence was through letters. Every time Dad's letters arrived[42] the neighbours would come to listen! How beautiful the place was; how nice the people are; how well organised the whole system is'.

Having arranged sufficient finance to purchase a house in Oldham town centre he then sent for his family to join him. However Bharat's mother was reluctant to leave India for an uncertain and alien life in Oldham and took a great deal of convincing that this was the right move. But eventually she agreed and Bharat arrived in Oldham aged ten in 1965 together with his mother, two elder sisters and a younger brother.

Bharat's father was a fluent English speaker as a result of working in the Indian Judicial system established under British Empire rules. This enabled him to advance rapidly while working in the mills. 'His first job was in Lily Mills, in Shaw. There were a large number of Asian people working there and a communication problem as not many could speak English. He became the personnel manager for the Asian workforce'.

'The intention was – when we came here – was to go back. Get education; earn money; and go back. But it never happened. Some people did go back but couldn't settle. After living here for some years they couldn't fit in over there. Mum didn't really like it here. She couldn't speak English. When we went to school and Dad went to work she was on her own. The weather never suited her; she was always saying 'let's go back'. After my Dad died she did go back to India for some time. But when we were married and expecting our first baby she came back and stayed, but would go back and forth'.

Bharat's father Jagatsingh became the pivotal figure in founding the Ashton and Oldham Indian Associations. 'My Dad organised the Indian Associations in Ashton, Oldham and Stalybridge. There was one for all the[43] community in Ashton. But following the expulsion by Idi Amin[44] of Ugandan Asians and others leaving from Kenya we had a large influx of Asian Indians coming from East Africa. About 150 families arrived[45] which was a large number compared to the two families when we arrived here'.

As the number of Indians grew in Oldham Jagatsingh set up an Oldham Indian Association. Without a local community centre or temple the first community activities and religious services took place at the Sisodia family home.

Jagatsingh died suddenly and unexpectedly in 1968 when Bharat was still in education. The unexpected death of his father had a huge impact on both Bharat's career plans and Oldham's Indian community. However Bharat was determined to continue the work of his father within the Indian community.

In 1972 funds were raised to buy a derelict Baptist Hall in Fern Street, Oldham and to convert it to a community centre. As the community grew the need for a temple became increasing urgent. The Fern Street centre was extended in 1974 and became the first Hindu temple in northern Greater Manchester. This was a real 'first' for Oldham – ahead of Rochdale, Tameside, Bolton and Bury. With Bharat working tirelessly together with many other dedicated committee members it was expanded but still did not provide sufficient space for all the community activities. In 1995 ambitious plans were announced for a purpose built centre and temple to be built on the site of the former Hathershaw public baths on Schofield Street. Over £600,000 was generated in four years of fund raising and the centre and temple opened in 1999 in a ceremony attended by over 1,500 people.

Bharat's intention had been to study medicine at university but that plan had to be abandoned following the death of his father. Instead he began work as an apprentice with British Telecommunications. There then followed a successful 20 year career in telecommunications. In the late 1990s, he took advantage of the restructuring of BT, and left to start a second career as a Financial Advisor with Allied Dunbar which later became the Zurich Advice Network (ZAN)[46].

As a result of his own successful business record and his close involvement with the Indian Association Bharat was invited to be one of the founding directors of the Asian Business Association.

'The ABA was set up to assist Asian business. We would guide them, help them whatever way we can. We would also tell them about our own experiences. These businesses started growing in Oldham and proved very successful'.

'The Board of Directors consisted of a mixture of Indians, Pakistanis, Bangladeshis. We never had any dispute. That was a unique thing. There was such a strong bond between all the directors. Sometimes we felt why can't the countries have this bond? If India, Pakistan and Bangladesh had this kind of relationship there would not be these wars; there would be peace, and happiness, and prosperity'.

SHREE RADHA KRISHNA TEMPLE
INDIAN ASSOCIATION
OLDHAM
COMMUNITY CENTRE

Second Generation

By the end of the 20th century Oldham's Asian business community was secure and confident. The 1990s had been a time of relative prosperity for Oldham as a whole and the town was beginning to face the next millennium with some confidence. Regeneration plans were in place to remove the grime and dereliction remaining from Oldham's industrial past; to sweep away areas of sub-standard terraced housing; and to further regenerate the improved town centre. Oldham's professional sports teams were doing well and there was an ambitious programme of investment in a Sports Park 2000 scheme and other leisure facilities. The wider economic base had diversified with office, health-service, higher and further education colleges and service industries all becoming important sectors in Oldham for the first time. The exclusively male Asian business community had changed as well.

The Female Entrepreneurs

Life for Oldham's Asian community in 2000 was radically different from that in the 1960s pioneer days, and nowhere was the difference more pronounced than for Asian women. Life was desperately hard for those early single males who came to work in the textile mills but it was equally hard for the wives and mothers of the early families. They remained confined in overcrowded and poor quality housing with no opportunity to acquire language skills or take up employment. Until the early mosques and community centres became established life must have been extremely isolated and unfulfilling. But the generation of women educated in Oldham could, and did, rise above these barriers to advancement.

Gita Chudasama

Making your way in business can be tough for anyone. Female entrepreneurs setting up in business face additional barriers posed by culture and gender – Asian females even more so. The achievement of Gita Chudasama is therefore truly inspirational.

Gita Chudasama left Gujarat in India in 1985 for an arranged marriage in Bolton. She arrived in England aged 23 unable to speak any English. As befits a Hindu bride her hands and arms were decorated with 'Mehndi[47]'. In a prescient foretaste of her future career the designs attracted a great deal of attention from fellow passengers. 'I couldn't speak a word of English and all the people on the plane next to me were English. I had henna on my hands, and they were so intrigued they asked me questions. Whether they understood my answers I don't know!'

Unfortunately the marriage was difficult and Gita, although she had been well educated in Gujarat and obtained a degree in physics, found her job opportunities limited due to her lack of fluency in English.

After two years Gita made her first separation from her husband and moved alone to Manchester to take a job in a Cash & Carry warehouse. 'It was broken English then. I was making a few sentences but by speaking to other English people[48] I picked it up. The other way I learned English was by watching television with sub-titles and reading English newspapers'.

Gita and her husband attempted reconciliation and by 1991 they had two children and had moved to Chadderton, Oldham to make a fresh start. However despite this the marriage once again broke down and Gita and the children were eventually abandoned in Chadderton.

Once her children were of school age, Gita, who had previously created henna designs and applications for family and friends, studied for a beauty therapy qualification at Oldham College. By 1997 she was divorced and had secured a job at a beauty salon in Manchester. After two years of working for someone else Gita was ready to start up her own business. With the help of a Business Start Up course at Falcon Enterprise and help from Anwar Choudhry of the Asian Business Association 'Precious Beauty' opened on 2 January 2000.

She found her premises in a true entrepreneurial style:

'I saw this empty house and thought I only live two minutes away from here. I put a note through the door asking them to ring me if they wanted to rent it'.

For the first two years the business did well and the property was situated conveniently close to home so that Gita could look after her children as well as the business. But it was in poor condition and the landlord would not carry out necessary repairs. With support from Oldham Chamber and the Asian Business Association Gita managed to surrender the lease on the old property and to purchase a better property in Burnley Lane, Chadderton. Established in her new premises Gita was able to develop her business. Now thirteen years on Precious Beauty is established as an award winning beauty therapy business. In 2002 she won the ABA 'Business Woman of the Year' award and in 2005 Precious Beauty was declared Oldham Town Partnership 'Retail Business of the Year'. In further recognition of her achievements, in 2006 Gita won an award for Outstanding Achievement in the Community.

Nazia Saleem

Nazia Saleem was born in Denmark in 1976 of parents originally from Jhelum, Pakistan. In 1978 the family moved to Oldham where Nazia's grandfather had a shop and lived in Chadderton. Her father worked night shifts at Greenfield Mill until the early 1980s when ill health triggered by the working conditions caused him to leave mill work and become a taxi driver. Nazia's earliest memories are of school and then mosque for two hours a day after school, lessons to learn Urdu, and playing outside with other children. Her mother, as with others of that generation, remained at home to care for the family.

'Women didn't use to drive but they would still go out into town to local shops. They didn't use to work much either. Many had come from Pakistan and they were limited by communication barriers. They weren't able to work whereas the next generation has grown up, it's become very common for them to work'.

Nazia married soon after leaving school and had two children but when the marriage ended in separation and divorce she went back to studying and started work in a pharmacy. 'I wanted to do the best for my children so I started studying when I started work in a pharmacy. I did the 'over the counter' course, then the dispensing course, and started the technician course'.

The next stage to becoming a fully qualified pharmacist meant full-time study at a university. This was not a realistic option as by this time Nazia had remarried and was planning to have more children. Her new husband who was an undertaker suggested that as she wanted to study and develop her career then she should become an embalmer.

'I said – embalmer! I can't do that! I could not see myself operating on people who have died. But I did want to carry on studying and if it wasn't going to be pharmacy I needed something else'. Nazia was eventually persuaded to observe an embalming session. There it became clear to her that though the embalming process was completely proper and professional it did not allow for many cultural and religious beliefs such as keeping bodies shrouded and females not mixing with males outside of their family.

'When my husband told me that there was no Muslim female embalmer in the whole of Britain I thought – you know what? I want to make a difference. Asian women and Muslim women, because of their faith, they keep themselves covered, and that's how we live. And when we die it's very important that this stays the same. I wanted to do it according to our religion, and you can only do that if you are a Muslim. That was my deciding point, and I enrolled onto the course'.

The British Institute of Embalmers (BIE) courses were available for study at nearby Huddersfield, and more importantly the course could be followed on a part time basis. Nazia continued to work full time in the pharmacy, and also had two more children whilst studying to become a fully qualified Member of the BIE.

The demand for her services was strong from the outset as many of the early Asian migrants to the UK wished to be buried in the country of their birth. It is a legal requirement for bodies to be embalmed when repatriated but before Nazia's qualification the embalming service could not be provided in accordance with Muslim beliefs. Nazia's unique achievement was reported in her local newspaper - the Oldham Advertiser - and the gaze of national media attention swiftly followed. She was invited to give a presentation at the Palace of Westminster after which the Diversity Group persuaded her to join the national Gender Equality and Racial Inclusion (GERI) project. The national GERI campaign seeks to

break down occupational stereotypes, challenge prejudice and promote equality and diversity.

'I was asked if I would take part in a selection of role models for Britain. It was to help inspire and motivate youth to new career pathways and eliminate stereotypical images. One hundred were selected and one was selected for a two page article in Diversity magazine – that was me! Then a DVD was made and circulated around schools'.

Today, though the demand for repatriation embalming has declined, Nazia's skills are still much in demand. She remains the only qualified female Muslim embalmer in the UK and prepares bodies for funeral presentation on behalf of families throughout the country. With what she describes as a stereotypical Muslim background Nazia understands better than most the difficulties faced by Asian women striving for a business career. Today she is a successful funeral director responsible for all aspects of bereavement services as well as continuing to use her unique skills in Muslim embalming.

Shurjahan Begum

Shurjahan Begum was born in Oldham in 1978 into a Bangladeshi family. Though she has visited Bangladesh several times she is very much a child of Oldham and could not envisage living back in her parents' country.

Her father had moved to Oldham in his 30s and lived a bachelor life sharing a crowded house with other working Asian males until his wife and Shurjahan's elder brother and sister could join him. He worked 12-hour night-shifts in textile mills while Shurjahan's mother was at home working as a clothing machinist.

The members of the Begum family demonstrate a strong entrepreneurial streak. Shurjahan, a talented cook and a quarter finalist on TV's Masterchef, worked in a variety of jobs from the age of 16, and in cooperation – and sometimes competition – with her brother experimented with a number of business ideas. It was 2004 when the first really successful business was established. In that year her brother Abdul Alim and sister Nurjahan created Nur76 – an international bestselling skin product. Nur76 is a market leading product selling in the United States, the UK and Europe, and many other parts of the World. The 76 refers to the 76th formulation of a 100% herbal, alcohol-free and animal product-free skin lightening cream now manufactured and marketed by UK Skin Lightening established and based in Oldham.

Shurjahan's first successful business was an online spice retail business. 'I was a very keen cook. I started[49] with spices I used to make, grind and label to sell on line. It did well, other than the house smelt of spices! I had a CD with instructions: how to use these spices; what ingredients to use; pictures of how the dish should look'. Competition began to increase from other spice suppliers and Shurjahan was limited in the quantities she could supply working from home. After two years she moved on from selling spices to find another business that she could operate from home.

That business turned out to be photography and since 2010 'Jahans Photography' has grown into a successful regional photography business. In the niche sector of an Asian female professional photographer Shurjahan is able to accommodate cultural and religious requirements across a range of communities.

'I do a lot of weddings, Mehndis[50] for a lot of cultures. The Hindu culture, the Sikh culture, Pakistani, Bengalis; white and traditional weddings'.

Shurjahan believes firmly that the business opportunities she has grasped in Oldham would not have been possible if her family had stayed in Bangladesh. She has been back to her parent's village several times, including spending a year there when she was younger. 'The life of a woman there is very different. Here I can get in my car; go shopping; buy my own things. I love that freedom and independence. Over there I couldn't go out to the bazaar and choose my own food, buy my own things. There would be name calling – look at this girl, this woman; she just goes out and shops; she is supposed to let her husband or father-in-law do it. There are a lot of restrictions. I was last there for three months and although I enjoyed the experience I was glad and happy to be home. When I am here I am so independent, and I love that freedom'.

The Female Entrepreneurs

The emergence of female Asian entrepreneurs marks a significant development for Oldham's Asian community. It is a development that would have been unthinkable back in the 1960s. Yet this development has been actively supported and encouraged by the Asian Business Community.

The numbers of female Asian entrepreneurs are growing and they are active in pharmacies, retail, catering, clothing and life style businesses. In many ways the female-owned businesses are at the same stage and following the same pathway as the early Asian male family businesses did in the 1970s.

The New Generation

The pace of change in technology and the wider business economy accelerates year-on-year and the latest generation of Asian entrepreneurs are part of this rush of speed towards progress. Born and raised in Oldham they do not share the thoughts of their earlier generations of 'home' being in Asia, or that their business activity in Oldham is in any way transient. The new generation is ambitious and seeking growth above settling for stability.

Wasim Aslam

Wasim Aslam is a third generation Asian businessman who was born and raised in Oldham. His grandfather was a pioneer Asian worker who left Pakistan for Peterborough in the 1960s. Wasim's mother and father were the next generation to leave Pakistan arriving in 1972. They were 25 and 18 years old when they arrived in Peterborough where Wasim's grandfather was already established. Work was readily available in a Post Office sorting depot but the need to support the growing family of three boys and a girl and the attraction of higher earnings led them to leave Peterborough after ten years to take up shift-work in cotton spinning at Elk Mill, Oldham.

Wasim was born in Coppice where he was raised and educated. Whilst studying at Tameside College in 1993 his eldest brother Nahim opened a new restaurant, Indian Ocean, in Ashton where Wasim worked part-time during his time as a student. Indian Ocean was at that time building a formidable reputation as one of

the North West's best restaurants, and to this day is regularly rated in the top 50 UK Curry restaurants.

After leaving college Wasim started work for Oldham Council as a housing officer but life in the local authority Housing Department seemed dull in comparison to the Indian Ocean and after two years as a housing officer Wasim went to work full time for his brother.

Eight years later in the aftermath of the 2001 Oldham disturbances Wasim took the opportunity to leave the Indian Ocean to start his own restaurant in Oldham. It was a brave decision for many in the town feared for the economic future of Oldham at this time. The site of Wasim's new venture, Café Lahore, was opposite the offices of The Oldham Chronicle in premises that had been damaged and then closed following the riots. However Café Lahore was to be no imitation of his brother's Indian Ocean restaurant which has a 100 person function room, over 40 staff and a full programme of live entertainment. Café Lahore is smaller and specialist, holding a unique position as Oldham's only Punjabi restaurant.

'It is a Punjabi and Kashmir cuisine. The food is a little bit different to a lot of restaurants in Oldham. There are only a handful of Punjabi restaurants in Manchester and Bradford. This is the only Punjabi and Kashmir restaurant in Oldham'.

There was a policy decision not to be licensed for alcohol. 'We don't have a bar in here. I don't feel comfortable working with alcohol, and I prefer not selling alcohol. We are surrounded[51] by bars and clubs and customers can go there. I can have a restaurant where people have not over done it'. The lack of a bar has not held the business back, and has enabled a cross-cultural clientele.

'We work on a 50:50 split – Asian and non-Asian. In the past there were a lot of ladies like my mum who stayed at home to raise the family. Now the trends have changed. Both females and males are working and don't have time to cook at home or want to come out for a meal by choice. There's a lot of young people who love going out and socialising with friends. It helps businesses and it helps people'.

Café Lahore has developed a thriving outside catering business delivering to and serving clients in Oldham, Stockport and Cheshire. The links with the Asian Business Association are very strong as the ABA helped Wasim to set up his business and as a consequence Café Lahore became the default meeting place for regular committee meetings. Wasim also readily acknowledges how important was the encouragement and help from his mother and brothers.

'When I bought the business I was introduced to the ABA and we have had a tight bond ever since. I've attended nearly every[52] function from when I started in business. The ABA has helped me through many hurdles: health and safety, customer service skills, staff training'.

Café Lahore has remained under Wasim's ownership for the last twelve years and over the last decade has received accolades in both local and national curry restaurant competitions. Wasim has won numerous business awards including 'Start up of the Year', 'Entrepreneur of the Year', and in 2008 'Oldham Business of the Year'.

Mashukul Hoque

Mashukul Hoque is one of the most successful of Oldham's third generation Asian entrepreneurs. His grandfather was the first of his family to leave Sylhet to find work in Britain and one of the very first immigrant pioneers. It was the UK's post World War Two labour shortage that offered employment to Mashukul's grandfather in 1951 and his first job was unloading ships in Liverpool docks.

Having learnt basic English in Pakistan Mashukul's grandfather had better opportunities in skilled work than were available to many, allowing him work in the North West textile industry. 'People who could speak a little bit of basic English, they were the ones who ended up working in the mills because there were health and safety considerations. Working in the docks usually meant just carrying things'.

By 1959 Mashukul's grandfather had settled in Oldham and had managed to save enough to buy a house. This made it possible for Mashukul's father to also travel to Oldham in search of work - by ship to Liverpool docks as had his father before him. 'The first house[53] my grandfather bought, he bought for £300. I was able to verify that figure as I saw the deeds'. Both grandfather and father worked in cotton and textile mills in Oldham and the surrounding areas. Family contact was minimal with visits back to Sylhet only possible every five years or so – but by air rather than sea.

It was 1974 before the family was re-united on a permanent basis when Mashukul, aged five and speaking no English, arrived with his mother and younger sister to stay in Oldham. By this time the family had gone into retail setting up a food and grocery store, Miah & Brothers, in Westwood, Oldham, on the site where a major food retailer is now located.

'As early as the late 1960s work in the factories was drying up. Transition had started with work going to other countries.

My family were quite aspirational; they saw factory work as a temporary thing. But setting up a business was hard. Though he[54] could speak English it wasn't to the degree that you could sit in front of a bank manager and go through a business proposal. The way to set up a business was to use any savings you had and ask your friends and relatives[55]. Bank loans and credit cards didn't exist. So my dad, uncle and grandad pooled their resources and managed to set up the shop. It was very successful. There were only three such shops in Oldham. It was that time[56] when people were setting up restaurants and takeaways for the first time. Customers came from Tameside, Manchester, even Leeds'.

Mashukul's early years in Oldham involved several moves around the borough mainly motivated by dissatisfaction with local schools. From Westwood the family moved to Failsworth in 1978, to Glodwick in 1991, then to Royton in 1995. 'I do remember it[57] was a rough area, with resentment building up from sections of the white community. The schools were all going downhill. I don't particularly have any bad memories of being in the school, but looking back that school was terrible. A lot of the teachers had openly racist attitudes'.

'The 1970s, that was my difficult period. It was that period when the National Front gained popularity. Looking back, a lot of it was to do with factories closing, looking for a scapegoat. My grandfather never mentioned any problems[58]. He used to talk about how friendly the white community was towards him - he had a lot of friends in the white community. How factory owners went out of their way to assist. The factory managers used to run very basic numeracy classes within the factory. When people wanted to buy houses, the factory would often help out, talk to the bank manager, give references, fill out applications and help them. My father told me about some of the issues he encountered but I remember myself, in the late 1970s, the police coming round on Saturday afternoon and advising us to shut the shop as the National Front were marching in the area'.

Mashukul's parents placed a high premium on education. 'They always encouraged me – in fact more than encouragement. There were some very strict rules on school having priority over everything else. There was no question of not going to university and I was one of the very first people from my community to go to university. I seem to recall that in 1989 Oldham Council did a survey of people going to university broken down by ethnic group. It listed three people from the Bangladeshi community – I must have been one of the three people!'

Mashukul went to Liverpool University to study computing on a three year degree course. He graduated in 1992, when there was a huge demand for people with computing skills. 'This was just at the start of mass computerisation in this country - mobile technology has just arrived. I graduated on a Friday, and had several job offers by the Monday!'

Mashukul worked for seven years for computing companies in Liverpool and London. In 1999 he set up his own company in Old Trafford – Sandyx Systems Ltd - which specialises in database integration services. The company has since diversified and has firmly established a niche as one of the UK's leading providers of cloud computing, systems integration, application development and support services.

His first contract was for the finance company GE Capital and they remain a client to this day. Other well known major companies were recruited by word of mouth and referrals, and the current client base reads like an extract from a FTSE Top 100 company list: Shop Direct Group, Salesforce, the Co-operative Group, DHL, Experian, Hermes Parcels, Linpac, BT, Speedy Hire in addition to Asda; Talk Talk; Eddie Stobart and Sainsburys.

Today, Sandyx is based in modern offices in Salford where consultants work with clients throughout Europe and with a development centre based in Banglalore, India.

Today's outsourcing of IT skills is an ironic reversal of the cotton industry's recruitment of immigrant workers – not for cost saving but to gain access to skills that are in short supply in the UK. 'It is a bit of a myth that you outsource to save money, you can't get these skills in this country. The universities in Banglalore are all sponsored by major IT companies. The world's biggest IT companies are now based in India'.

The Oldham Asian Business Association has not played a significant part in Mashukul's business career. 'I don't have any particular connection to the Oldham ABA. I did go to the inaugural meeting, and I am aware of what they do. I am in a very strange business sector, so, not in a demeaning way, there is nothing for me to gain. They have got some good services and I know they help a lot of businesses'.

As a third generation entrepreneur Mashukul has clear views on what the business future could look like. 'The big trend that I've noticed is that people are diversifying into all types of different businesses. The big growth seems to be in things that people from our background are interested in. At the moment some of the wealthiest people from the Indian sub-continent that have settled here are in property and travel. Financial services is the one that is really growing at the moment'.

He expects his business to continue
to grow.

'The timing is right for the
business to grow more rapidly
than it has in the past. What I
would like to see in ten years
time is that the business has
crossed certain thresholds - in
revenue and the number of
staff. I will be working on the
business, not in the business,
in a chairman-type role'.

As for the next generation of Asian
entrepreneurs that chapter has yet to be
written. But if Mushukul's son is any
indication the future is bright. At age 16
his son is emerging as one of the UK's
most promising motorsport drivers. Having
been a talented kart racer since age seven,
he is setting lap records throughout the
country and competing at the highest
levels of junior motorsport throughout the
UK and Europe. He has his sights firmly set
on Formula One.

Business support in
Oldham and the Asian
Business Association

Excellence Awards
7th Annual Business Awards
ellence and Achievements
Business of the Year
Retail Business of the Year

Business support in Oldham and the Asian Business Association

The emergence of ethnic minority businesses as a significant sector of the British economy was not predicted or even recognised at the time. In the 1990s the Department of Trade & Industry (DTI) was focused almost exclusively on large business and operated with the definition of a small firm as 'one with fewer than 250 employees'. Even in the 1990's that definition would identify any such employer as a major employer and in the top 30 employers in Oldham.

The DTI's limited resource for helping small businesses was the Small Firm's Advisory Service (SFAS) staffed by businessmen who had mostly retired from large business organisations. The SFAS advisors with few exceptions offered no understanding of small business culture. To serve the whole of the North West there was one part-time SFAS business adviser with Asian language ability and cultural awareness whose main employment was as an accountancy lecturer at Staffordshire Polytechnic. This scarce resource had no impact on the development of Asian businesses in Oldham.

The private sector business establishment was equally slow off the mark to recognise the growth of ethnic minority, primarily Asian businesses. The Bank of England published 'The Financing of Ethnic Minority Firms in the United Kingdom' in 1999 which noted for the first time and at least a decade late that 'the contribution of ethnic minority firms to the UK economy as a whole is considerable and represents a growing part of the small business market'. The report went on to note that in 1997 the rate of ethnic minority business start-ups at 9% was almost double the 5% proportion of the UK's Asian population and that in the UK as a whole 7% of all small businesses were ethnic minority owned.

The situation in Oldham was markedly ahead of the national provision. Oldham Enterprise Agency took over responsibility for encouraging small business development from the SFAS in 1990

and set out to provide services for Asian businesses. Business population data only existed at regional level in 1990 and was notoriously incomplete. Oldham Enterprise estimated that there were about 3000 effective full time businesses in Oldham Borough and that about 10% of Oldham's business population was of ethnic ownership.

Daood Akraam from Oldham was recruited and trained as a self-employed business advisor contracted to Oldham Enterprise Agency. Born in Oldham in 1966 of Pakistani parents Daood was an active and able business adviser who provided the first Asian-specific business support services in Oldham. He then went on to set up his own consultancy business, served on the board of the Asian Business Association and was a central adviser to the development of the Rushholme Traders Association and Manchester's famous Curry Mile.

In 1991 Oldham's pre-eminent businessman, Norman Stoller of Seton Healthcare Group, headed the successful establishment of the Oldham Training and Enterprise Council (Oldham TEC) that took over responsibility for government funded business services. One of their first actions was to undertake a local business census to provide accurate Oldham area economic data for the first time. There were 304 Asian businesses identified which together with other minority businesses – Ukrainian, Chinese, Afro-Caribbean – took the proportion of Oldham ethnic minority businesses comfortably over the 10% estimate.

Under Norman Stoller's chairmanship support for the growing Asian business sector and the eventual formation of the Asian Business Association was given the highest priority. In 1993 a combined initiative by Oldham TEC, Oldham Enterprise Agency and the local authority developed a managed workspace facility in a redundant velvet mill - the Falcon Enterprise Centre in Chadderton.

It was at the Falcon Centre in 1993 that Anwar Choudhry was appointed 'Ethnic Minority Business Counsellor', the first full-time post serving Oldham's Asian business community. Anwar worked full time with Asian businesses in Oldham for almost eighteen years in a number of different capacities but always in close liaison with the ABA since its formation in the 1990s. He is one of the two most influential people in this history of Asian business growth in Oldham along with Tariq Amin, the first chair and life President.

Anwar was born in 1952 in Pakistan. His family moved to the UK and settled in Doncaster. His family home remains in Doncaster but he effectively lived in Oldham from 1993 to 2011. He then returned to Doncaster to run his consultancy business. In between he held business consultant and adviser posts with Oldham Borough Council, Oldham Chamber of Commerce, and Business Link NW. From 2000 to 2008 he worked directly for the Asian Business Association as Business Support Manager.

Anwar had managed a number of businesses in his 20s and 30s before obtaining his BA degree in Public Administration at Sheffield Hallam University as a mature student. His first impressions of Oldham in 1993 were not favourable. 'It was a bit of a shock compared to Doncaster. A lot worse to what I was used to but it was a challenge as well - to make a difference'. He felt it was an advantage to have this outside perspective and not to come from the local area.

Anwar Choudhry

'There were two large communities, the Pakistanis and the Bangladeshis, and also the Indian community but with a smaller number of businesses. I quickly became aware and learned there were various groups within the communities. However one of the distinct advantages I had as an outsider was to keep an impartial viewpoint. Most of the early businesses I came across were largely retail groceries. Then takeaways and restaurants began to develop and grow'.

Many of the businesses setting up in catering had to deal with food hygiene regulations for the first time and most were being started by people with English as a second language.

Therefore 'it became a bit of a major issue in terms of delivering the training[59]. To address this problem I enrolled at Oldham College to get a teacher training qualification. I then obtained the Advanced Food Hygiene Certificate so as to qualify as a trainer with the Chartered Institute of Environmental Health. As a result I could deliver the training without an interpreter in a number of community languages'.

This was a ground breaking innovation at a national level and food hygiene training became a mainstay of ABA service delivery. It also paved the way for Asian businesses to see the value of training and qualifications for their workforce which would support the emergence of businesses of greater sophistication and technological prowess.

A further landmark for the ABA was the growth of its annual business awards and dinners. Business dinners had a track record of being well attended in Oldham and the Oldham Chamber in the late 1990s had some of the best attended business events in the North West albeit with only minor involvement of Asian businesses. However by 2001 Government policy changes had removed ninety million pounds of annual funding for business services and the Chamber was in terminal decline. The ABA decided to hold their first dinner and awards event in the autumn of 2001, the year in which the Oldham riots took place over a May Bank Holiday.

'There were negative perceptions about the BME community - benefit scroungers and so on. One of the ways we could eradicate this was through creating awareness, that there is a dynamic business community here contributing to the local economy and employing large numbers of people'.

The 2001 business award dinner went a long way to helping retrieve Oldham's business confidence and set the template for a succession of bigger and better dinners that were multicultural and eventually eclipsed the other business dinners organised in the borough.

'The first dinner in 2001 attracted about 280 people. We learnt quite a lot from that, and with the Chamber dinner declining the ABA dinner and awards started increasing year by year. What I wanted to do was to demonstrate the positive aspects of Asian business in the Oldham Borough and to celebrate their achievements in order to encourage other budding entrepreneurs. Also I wanted to create a platform where businesses and other professionals, from both the public and the private sectors, could meet in an 'informal setting' affording networking situations and contributing to community cohesion. As a result it wasn't just the Asian businesses who were at the dinner and award ceremonies but something like 50% of the attendees were from the indigenous business community'.

The event grew in strength year-by-year until the only limitation was the size of Oldham's largest venue, the Queen Elizabeth Hall, which could cater for a maximum of 450 people. The present successor is the 'One Oldham' Business Awards, a highly successful multicultural business awards dinner.

In the early 2000s Oldham and the Asian Business Association was seen as a national exemplar of multicultural good practice. Together with similar organisations in Leicester, Birmingham and Bolton, Oldham was the model to follow for multicultural business development. The decision to wind down the ABA seems exactly right to Anwar.

'A new generation of entrepreneurs are coming through where language is not so much of an issue. That level of support and hand-holding is not required. The ABA has fulfilled its function and now the dynamics are different. It is a natural progression and that is why an informed decision was made by ABA Board members to call it a day'.

'I was involved hands on, drawing on my practical business experience. I was offering practical advice. Some took it on board and some didn't. Those that did are still going strong, have developed and not only bettered themselves in the nicest possible way but have also made positive contributions to Oldham's economy. As someone who was involved from almost the beginning to the end, the ABA has become part and parcel of Oldham's social history as well as business history'.

Another individual, Kashif Ashraf, has been an integral part of the ABA and its work. Kashif is the epitome of third generation Oldham Asian entrepreneurs. Born in Oldham in 1968 he was one of the first graduates from a Pakistani heritage background to work in Oldham as a professional when he joined the then Careers Service in 1992. As a result he was seen as an ideal partner by Oldham Coliseum Theatre Board, the Racial Equality Partnership, Oldham College Board and more recently Mahdlo Youth Zone and the Oasis Academy Board who were all keen to engage with the rapidly emerging Asian new generation.

Kashif Ashraf

This spread of contacts also made Kashif an extremely effective networker mediating between the Asian Business Association and member businesses but also with ABA partner and friend organisations such as the Chamber of Commerce, Business Link, Oldham Council and the Business Leadership Group.

Kashif's parents arrived in Oldham from Pakistan attracted by the ready availability of work. His mother, the daughter of Mohammed Amin founder of Amin Poultry, arrived in the early 1960s and became one of the first interpreters for the National Health Service in the 1980s. Kashif's father, Mohammed Ashraf, came to Oldham in 1968 and set up electronics and mobile phone businesses.

Surrounded by business-minded and ambitious family members an early upbringing in business became a routine way of life. 'I can remember as a young boy of eight or nine my grandad and uncle used to take me with them in the van even if it was just holding the calculator while they made deliveries. It was a good way of learning and understanding. And then when my Dad set up in business[60] I would help my Dad out after college or on weekends and evenings. Not because he asked me to but because I wanted to'.

Kashif experienced first hand how the generation of Asian entrepreneurs born in Oldham has influenced the growth of Asian businesses. 'Every child throughout our business history has added some value to the family business. When computers first came along my uncle, Rahil, introduced computing into the business whilst he was still at college'.

His grandfather Mohammed Amin started retailing poultry in the 1960s but saw no reason not to diversify when he spotted an opportunity. He was close to the 'rag trade' – the cut, make and trim of fashion garments – which boomed in central Manchester in the 'swinging' sixties. In visits to Holland to source new suppliers of poultry for the fast growing Amin Poultry business he realised the price differential for clothing particularly from 'Cool Britannia'. So he drove van-loads of Manchester fashion clothing to Holland for sale via Dutch market traders. This eye for an entrepreneurial opportunity was echoed by Kashif in 2000.

His wife Sabeen had opened a clothes shop in Oldham aimed at the latest Asian fashion market. Kashif and best friend Muzahid Khan spent their weekends driving to London's East End to return with the newest fashion stock for the shop. 'We made some contacts in London[61] and me and my friend Muzahid would drive all the way to London, buy the stock and drive it back. We were successful because no one else did this and women wanted something different. We would ring up people on the way back about the stock

that was about to land in the shop. By the time we got there customers were at the shop excited to buy the clothes'.

Kashif was involved with the emerging Asian Business Association in a unique way, not as a business owner, but as the liaison person between the then current business, education and local government organisations.

'Though I was working in a professional job[62] and not running a business in my own right I became an honorary member of the ABA. From it's inception to the present day I have always been there. In 1992 there weren't many Pakistanis or Bangladeshis in professional roles in Oldham. I got picked up by different organisations like Oldham College and the Council and began to go on boards. The first Asian businesses were self employed - taxi drivers, takeaways, restaurants, some clothing trades. Now it has expanded into all types of services. It has had a massive impact on the town because of their[63] entrepreneurial spirit driving the town forward. The Asian Business Association has been a good bunch of people that tried to make the town better for the whole community – not just the Asian community'.

This aspiration was temporarily threatened by the Oldham riots of late May 2001. Disturbances occurred in Coppice, Westwood and Chadderton but were particularly intensive in Glodwick to the south of Oldham town centre. Here the use of petrol bombs, bricks, and bottles by Asian youths as they battled far right protesters and the police were vividly captured by TV and media video crews. No one was killed though at least 20 people were injured in the riots and 37 people were arrested. The damage in financial terms to property was surprisingly minimal but the real damage was from the media footage televised around the world.

Though only a small area of the town was affected by the three days of riots, Oldham's reputation as a whole suffered a serious set-back. Local businesses had long-standing supply contracts terminated by national and international purchasers worried about disruption of supply. Many businesses found it prudent to replace Oldham with Greater Manchester in their address and marketing literature. Tensions between the white and Asian communities led to accusations of a sales boycott and the previously vibrant town centre night time economy crashed to a halt.

'When the Oldham's riots happened it did affect businesses from two points of view. It affected the businesses based in the riot areas and it affected many businesses in terms of friction between Asian and white communities. But when the riots happened it was Asian businesses going out calming people down. They took responsibility for things that were going on so business leaders were out speaking to people trying to sort out the issues arising from the riots'.

From the low point of 2001 Kashif argues that Asian businesses are today a major economic force for good. 'The history of Oldham shows that as businesses became established[64] these business people started building schools, building libraries. Asian businesses only really started to flourish in the 1970s and 80s when the people running them were in their thirties and forties. Now, in 2012, those people are 60 or 70. They have been successful in business and what is natural is philanthropic work. In terms of the Asian Business Association I don't see it as an end but a new beginning. Those board members are moving onto different boards or are involved in different things. The idea of leaving a legacy has come about with donations to Oldham Sixth Form College, to Oldham College, and to other educational institutions in Oldham. Every year there will be an Enterprise Prize so the legacy will be living on'.

Big Business success from small local beginnings

Iqbal Ahmed and Ajit Medtia

Iqbal Ahmed and Ajit Medtia are two Oldham born Asian business people that cannot be omitted from any record of Asian business growth in Oldham. I have met and talked with both of them over the years but was unable to interview them specifically for Cotton, Curry and Commerce.

These case histories are partially based on my own recollections but draw heavily on an obituary for Ajit Medtia written by Carl Marsden for the Oldham Advertiser and Manchester Evening News and a feature article on Iqbul Ahmed written by Shelina Begum for the Greater Manchester Business Week in January 2013. Grateful acknowledgement is given for permission to reproduce quotations from, and extracts of, these articles.

Ed Stacey

Ajit
Medtia

Property tycoon, film maker and Indian prince

Oldham-born Ajit Medtia founded the Red Lion Construction and Medtia Development companies that were behind numerous developments in Oldham Borough. Ajit became a property millionaire, married an Indian princess, played polo with Prince Charles and funded a film – Chicken Tikka Masala - that became a box office hit. It was a great shock when he tragically died from cancer in 2008 at the age of 39. By then he had made a major mark on his hometown. His self-built company, Medtia Associates, was behind a number of office and commercial developments in Oldham. He held the office of Vice Chairman of the Oldham Asian Business Association from inception until 2002.

Ajit Medtia's insatiable thirst for proving his worth resulted in the creation of a business empire that had made him a millionaire by the age of 29. With the looks of a Bollywood leading man and an Indian princess for a wife, acquaintances recall him as an extrovert and flamboyant man

who made an indelible mark on all who met him. The Medtia family's local connections began when Ajit's barrister grandfather came to Oldham during the postwar cotton boom.

Ajit was born at the Royal Oldham Hospital but his early childhood was split between Oldham and his grandfather's estate in Gujarat, northern India. His family were landed gentry in Rajasthan with farm and quarry interests.

Ajit became head boy at Grange School in Oldham before studying civil and structural engineering at Imperial College, London. His first career was in merchant banking but he opted out to build his own company. Returning to Oldham around 1990 he set up Red Lion Construction.

'It was a personal point to prove to my father that I could do it on my own', he said. 'Our first job was a small extension where the house owner knew more than we did. We then went on to a £25,000 job and an industrial unit for £68,000,

then a nursing home. I was lucky in that I managed to invest in Oldham at a time when property prices were very low and the town centre was not going anywhere'.

Ajit's firm began investing and building locally even after the 'flight' of national property investors following the Oldham's riots of 2001. To this day a series of town centre development sites bear the 'Medtia' prefix in their name.

In his personal life Ajit's aunt introduced him to a woman in Bombay in 1994 that she thought would be a good match. Princess Shruti Kumari is the sister of the Maharajah of Karauli in eastern Rajasthan. Her predecessors had ruled an area of more than 1,200 square miles from 1100 until 1947 when India gained independence. Their lavish one-week wedding ceremony in January 1995 was attended by around 2,000 guests. To some astonishment the couple then returned to live in a four bedroom Victorian house in Werneth, a humble lifestyle Shruti appeared to relish.

'We do not hold official titles in India anymore', she said. 'It's quite nice just leading a normal life. At times the limitations and restrictions of being a royal can be overbearing'. Ajit, his wife and two children moved to London in 2002 where he continued to develop and diversify his interests. As a descendant of the Rathore Rajputs from the Jodphur dynasty, he also had the sport of polo in his blood and after learning to ride from scratch in later life set up his own 'Red Lions' team in Cheshire. Ajit went on to fulfill a long held ambition of playing in a team alongside Prince Charles in 2003.

Wherever his jet-set lifestyle took him, however, Medtia always held his home-town close to his heart. In 1999 he was asked why he had uprooted his new wife to Werneth. He said 'I just have an affinity for the town. You can walk down the street in Oldham, ask someone the time and they'll tell you the time and their life story'.

Iqbal Ahmed

£250m seafood empire began in a Glodwick shop

The Seamark Group employs 400 staff in East Manchester, and has offices in London and New York. They sell more than 1,000 products including seafood, poultry, fruit and vegetables in Europe, the United States and Australia. The group has 4,000 employees in Bangladesh in three state of the art food processing plants served by a four strong fleet of fishing trawlers. The Seamark Group includes the exclusive and highly successful Vermilion Restaurant near the Etihad Stadium. This success has turned Iqbal into one of the UKs richest men. He is the highest ranked British Bangladeshi to feature on the Sunday Times Rich List. This international business empire started from a corner shop in Glodwick in the 1960s. As Oldham's most successful Asian businessman, he was the obvious choice to give the keynote speech at the launch of the Asian Business Association in May 1998.

Iqbal's father, Al-Haj Abdul Khalis, came to Oldham from Bangladesh in the 1960s and worked in textile mills until he had saved enough money to buy a shop in Glodwick. Iqbal, driven from Sylhet by war, arrived in Oldham aged 15 in October 1971 and he wasn't impressed! 'It was a foggy evening and we could hardly see anything. To me everyone looked alien wearing heavy clothes and hats on their heads. It was cold and my hands were freezing. I found the terraced houses very strange. They were small and made me feel claustrophobic. In Bangladesh we had a village house set in several acres of land'.

Iqbal studied business management at London City College and returned to Oldham in 1977 by which time his father's corner shop was well established in Glodwick. His mother was probably the first Asian lady to work in an Oldham shop.

However while Iqbal was working in London his father became ill and Iqbal returned to Oldham to help run the shop. Iqbal was ambitious and saw possibilities beyond just a local shop. He began to

supply fresh food and meat products to restaurants in Manchester and the North West, and then saw the potential of importing tropical fruit and vegetables. His first import was mangoes from Pakistan flown in by Lufthansa. 'It was our first exotic food. It worked so well I got in contact with friends in Bangladesh and told them I wanted Bangladeshi vegetables'.

He then found a supplier of seawater fish and introduced tiger prawns to the UK market. Up to this point IBCO, Iqbal Brothers Company, was based in Park Road, Oldham, but in 1982 the need for extra space and cold storage resulted in an expansion and relocation to larger premises in Clayton just outside the Oldham area.

The subsequent growth in exports led to a new company being formed, Seafood Marketing International PLC, trading as Seamark. The new name was in response to how the name Iqbal was perceived abroad. 'The difficulty we had was the name Iqbal Brothers. People asked too many questions about where we were from rather than what we had to sell. People sometimes found it difficult to believe that an Asian man was running a successful business. It never made me feel angry; I always saw it as a challenge'.

In 1991 Seamark opened their first processing factory in East Manchester, expanding in 1997 into a seven-acre site in Droylsden. In 2000 a £10m fish processing plant was opened in Chittagong, Bangladesh with Princess Anne as guest of honour. In 2004 Seamark developed a further six and a half-acre site in Eastlands near the Etihad Stadium home of Manchester City.

Iqbal's brothers and children manage various parts of the Seamark £250m international business. 'The challenge now is to remain successful. We have younger blood taking the business forward with their own vision. I want the next generation to continue the legacy my father started'.

Oldham's Business Community -

The old order changes

Oldham's Business Community -
The old order changes

Oldham's business community in the 1960s and 70s was a small, stable paternalistic melange with all the characteristics of a ruling establishment and the strengths and weaknesses implied therein. It was an exclusive inner circle that saw it as their job to 'do' things to Oldham rather than 'for' Oldham. Anyone outside of this group was perceived to be part of the problem.

At the time Oldham still had a small number of big manufacturing employers such as Ferranti, British Aerospace, Courtaulds, Seddon Atkinson, Seton Healthcare, Coin Controls, and Cobden Chadwick. These businesses which remained in local ownership or retained a strong local autonomy were actively and positively engaged in fighting Oldham's economic corner. They were supported by numerous small, under-resourced but fiercely proud and independent trade and business organisations - the Chamber of Commerce, Chamber of Trade, Engineering Training Association, Export Club, Enterprise Agency - and trade specific groups such as the Master Bakers, Butchers, Oldham Law Association, etc.

The main banks - Barclays, Lloyds, National Westminster, Midland – all had powerful local decision making independence unfettered by software-based assessment or regional offices. Though business rivals the bank managers met and networked with a commonality of purpose - to encourage economic growth or at least to prevent further decline.

The Oldham Chronicle was the only media organisation in Oldham with Fred Bottomley's[65] business pages required reading for anyone who was serious about business. Advertising - marketing was a new and uncertain concept at the time – was all channelled through the paper. In legal and accountancy services a handful of long established practices dominated Oldham's professional services sector.

Local government had been reorganised in 1974 resulting in a reluctant coalition of previously independent townships. Chadderton, Shaw and Crompton, Failsworth, Royton, Lees, and Saddleworth, all previously centres of political control and business activity, now found themselves dominated by the new Oldham Metropolitan Borough Council.

Given this mix of independent and free spirits the unsurprising governance style was top-down benevolent direction.

Oldham's establishment movers and shakers were few enough in number to be gathered in one room and around one table to sort out Oldham's problems. The overarching strategy was to save big manufacturing employers or to attract inward investment by offering land, buildings and a workforce with sufficient elementary education to ensure survival. Almost alone amongst the other Greater Manchester mill town areas Oldham persisted in membership of the

North of England Development Agency and in running a big-budget marketing strategy. This culminated in 'The Town in the Country' advertising campaign with national media adverts, 'Industrious Oldham' exhibitions, high profile investor events at the House of Commons, and London underground poster campaigns. The campaign was highly regarded locally but had absolutely no effect on inward investment. Any footloose companies looking to invest in North West England compared the high incentives and new-town infrastructure of green-field areas such as Warrington, Skelmersdale and North Wales with Oldham's haphazard industrial revolution mix of residential and semi-derelict factories and mills and chose not to come to Oldham.

Nationally the Government sought to promote business and enterprise through two Civil Service departments: the Department of Trade and Industry, and the Manpower Services Commission. These Westminster-based bureaucracies paid little attention to the Oldham economy. It was not depressed enough to warrant any real focus of attention and neither was local industry of sufficient strategic importance.

It was not until 1991 that these Government programmes and budgets were devolved to local control via the business community-led Training and Enterprise Councils (TECs). Oldham was one of the first TECs to be approved and one of the first actions to be undertaken was an economic assessment of the Oldham economy. It was slowly dawning on the Oldham business collective that their vision of the Borough as the major manufacturing area for North Manchester was neither possible nor desirable. Instead investment in education, up-skilling the workforce, improved transport links and new activities such as information technology, financial services, healthcare, food and hospitality, tourism and the growth of a large number of small businesses was perceived as a potential way forward. In this new strategy the emerging Asian businesses that the established business community knew so little about would have an important part to play.

The view from inside

Michael Meacher MP came to Oldham in 1968 and has served as an Oldham MP since 1970. A passionate and loyal campaigner for Oldham he has the distinction of serving as a minister in the Wilson, Callaghan and Blair Labour governments. More than any other person he has witnessed and shaped the changes in Oldham over the last 43 years. In April 2013 he was elected an Honorary Freeman of the Borough.

He was the guest of honour for the official launch of the Asian Business Association on May 15th 1998 and is uniquely placed to comment on the contribution of the Asian business community. 'My earliest memories are of a town which was very poor. People were well below the national average[66] and dependent on fairly low pay, low skill jobs. We did not have the M62 or M6[67] at that time so it was difficult to get investment into Oldham. It remained very much a backwater industrially for the first 20 or 30 years I was an MP'.

'It all changed about 10 or 15 years ago and - I hate to say this - that it was significantly, not wholly, to do with the serious riot in 2001. It wasn't a race riot though it was assumed to be Asians versus whites but it wasn't. I was there in Glodwick[68]. It was a beautiful day, very calm and pleasant. I was woken the next day to be told there had been a riot. I couldn't believe it. It was a riot that clearly reflected gradual grievances that became more serious and then flared up. The BNP were in town[69] and you might have thought the BNP caused it but they didn't. They did introduce an air of menace, an atmosphere of threats and intimidation'.

'The significance was afterwards. It didn't happen immediately for no Government will say if you riot we are going to invest in your town. But that's what actually happened. We had more investment in the first ten years of the century than we had had in the previous thirty'.

'The children of the original settlers from Bangladesh and Pakistan grew up in this country or were born here. A number of those clearly had natural business instincts. They worked hard, and sometimes put the indigenous population to shame by working long hours and being diligent'.

'They had an instinct of what was needed, what would sell. They were prepared to invest their money in it. Some of them have been extraordinarily successful. Now they are central to the industrial backbone of Oldham. It is a community that is pretty dynamic, thrusting, ambitious, active and vibrant'.

'King Cotton was based on low wages and without the opportunity for people to rise to a higher station. It didn't have the creative opportunities which now have been taken advantage of by the younger generation. There has been a profound change in Oldham consistent with the rise of the Asian community. To a large degree they have driven it. It is not something that has just happened and they have just surfed the wave. They have created the momentum themselves'.

The emergence of Asian businesses in the 1970s was very much under the radar of the established business community. They were self-funded within the community without recourse to banks, accountants or professional advisers. These early Asian businesses worked long hours for often minimal return to make the businesses work and had little time for traditional business networking via trade associations, Round Table, and golf clubs.

The banking establishment

Of the banks that eventually developed an Asian business customer base, the Midland Bank was perhaps the most active. Steve Grant was based in Oldham and is the banking professional most closely associated with the Asian Business Association. He saw first hand how Asian businesses developed.

'I was the junior in the lending team dealing with lower value commercial propositions. Many of these would be for shops as that was the area at the time[70] that the Asian Community was moving into. The first one that came across the desk was a corner shop. He was a hard-working gentleman who was who was coming up to retirement age. He had built up cash and wanted to see that his family were right. At this stage there were no other jobs to go to in the mills and he wanted to provide for his family. He saw that this opportunity to purchase a traditional corner shop was the way forward'.

'The way the bank was approached by the Asian Community was different. The proposition would be less structured. There wouldn't be a business plan. There wouldn't be a cash flow forecast. I have X amount of cash; I want to buy the business; please lend me the money. It was as simple as that. We did lending then that would be impossible now. Back then, there was a lot more judgemental lending. The lending we did turned out to be very successful, very few propositions went wrong'.

Steve Grant's banking career took him away from Oldham in 1989 but he returned ten years later this time as manager with the bank now part of HSBC. 'The businesses in 2000 were totally different from when I had left. The whole thing had evolved into more complex businesses: into service industries, restaurants, higher value retail operations, larger scale manufacturing. The businesses started to develop into new areas, into more mature businesses that could provide employment not just for the family'.

'There are other towns – traditional cotton or textile towns – which didn't have the same degree of development and they haven't performed to the same level. It is down to the individuals who wanted to take things forward. The committee of the Asian Business Association had a wide remit of businesses and that business base helped them to lead and show others'.

'There are probably three or four Asian businesses[71] which are now multi-million [pound] businesses. But there are a lot of businesses that do good business. You don't have to be multi-million pound to be a business producing a good income and employing people'.

The new business establishment

The watershed for the Oldham business establishment came in 1991 when Oldham was included in the first wave of Training & Enterprise Councils (TEC) to be set up. Seventy-six TECs were established in England and Wales considerably more than the 40 or 50 bodies that Government had envisaged when it conceived the policy of devolving central government business programmes to local control.

It was down to the energy and persistent lobbying of local business men led by Norman Stoller of Seton Health Care that Oldham achieved single area TEC status. The Government had hoped for a Bolton/ Oldham/Rochdale TEC - derisively nicknamed 'Bochdale' by local opponents - but the proposal was vigorously resisted by these proud, independent and competing industrial towns.

Oldham TEC was at first mainly staffed by civil servants seconded from Government Regional Offices. It was not until the appointment of John Gracie as Chief

Executive in 1994 that the culture changed from that of a local civil service office delivering central government programmes. John had extensive private sector experience including dealing with the notorious print unions, restrictive practises, over-manning, resistance to new technology and so on.

With the firm backing of Norman Stoller and a board of local business leaders John set about merging and integrating the disorderly jumble of small, competing and overlapping business organisations that had characterised the Oldham business establishment. By 1995 the Oldham Chamber of Commerce, Training & Enterprise (OCCTE) had been formed. Despite this unwieldy title OCCTE was a genuine one-stop shop offering the complete range of business services in Oldham. With a ten million pound budget, local discretion on how to use that budget and a staff of around a hundred people OCCTE had the 'can do' culture, resources and expertise to set about Oldham's economic decline. At last Oldham had a business organisation of sufficient scale to work with Oldham Council on an equal footing rather than as a poor and dependent relative. For the first time, here was an organisation that recognised the potential of Asian businesses and that had the resources to help realise that potential.

OCCTE was one of the most successful TECs in England achieving the highest level of membership and business engagement. Many of the other TECs, particularly in London and the South East, failed to deliver on the same scale. Then, following an election and change of Government in 2001, all TECs including OCCTE, were abolished and Government policy swung back to centralised control through the Learning & Skills Council. As a result substantial amounts of funding disappeared from business support programmes altogether.

For Oldham the OCCTE ten year period was one of prosperity and advancement, a relative boom time compared to the gloom of the 1980s. John Gracie looks back at this time as one of the most fulfilling in his career. 'When I was appointed Oldham TEC was run like a government department offering government programmes. Oldham had a number of small business organisations which were weak and not doing much for the area. The objective for me was to pull all those things together'.

'In trying to offer business support services we were not reaching ethnic minority businesses. The Asian Business Association was a way of enabling that to happen. Having an ABA gave a route for that to happen, to get more people involved in the chamber. It went very well, right from the start. There was a lot of enthusiasm for it from all sectors. It wasn't just Pakistan, Bangladesh, India, it was all sectors'.

'Michael Meacher came to the launch[72] which was significant. As a chamber we were well supported by our local MPs. He was a Government Minister with lots of demands on his time, yet he came. The view of the OCCTE Board was that it was a top priority – as it was also of the people managing the business. We had been very successful in most of the things we did but there was one[73] where we hadn't been successful. It was very important and there was tremendous support from the Board.'

The view from outside

The main newspaper for the Oldham area is the Oldham Evening Chronicle founded in 1854. During the period covered by this book there were just two business correspondents: Fred Bottomley (1960 to 1991) and Martyn Torr (1991 to the present day). As well as reporting on the business community Martyn is also a director of Oldham's leading public relations and business event management company, New Image Ltd. New Image Ltd has organised most of the business events in Oldham since the 1990s and has worked closely with the Asian Business Association.

As the Chronicle business correspondent Martyn's brief was to cover all business sectors, not just indigenous traditional businesses. 'We covered everything – Asian businesses, West Indian, Chinese, Ukrainian – for Oldham had a sizable Ukrainian population way before the Asian community. I've not yet met an Asian businessman who is not seriously ambitious. They are driven people. If they have to work a bit longer that's fine. They think about business, business, business. It's an ethos that I think comes from their parents. If they weren't working in the mill they were working in the corner shop. They worked every hour God sent'.

'Some are extremely ambitious. I remember Ajit Medtia when he bought his first Ferrari. He drove it to our office with a box of cakes and took us out one by one for a drive in it and we all had a cake. He was so proud of it! He now has got his name all over Oldham: Medtia Square, Medtia Place, Medtia House. He has left a legacy'.

New Image Ltd has a particular specialism in organising large business dinners. The business dinner of the year in Oldham was the Chamber dinner which was organised by Martyn's New Image company for more than 20 years seating at it's zenith over 500 people at a formal dinner. When OCCTE was abolished the Asian Business dinner took over. It started from modest beginnings as Martyn vividly remembers.

'The ABA decided to hold a first dinner. At seven o'clock with the event due to start in half an hour they phoned needing some kit for the stage. We rushed round, saw they had very little, suggested this and that and put up a full stage set. Fortunately the event did not start on time! Our fee was to attend the dinner, have a free meal and then take our kit home. At the end of the event we said: next year, why don't you talk to us? In fairness to them, they did. It went from – chaotic is not the right word – an event stitched together to a very professional, very slick event with video screen relays, big name speakers and well known comperes. It became a huge event'.

Martyn's career in journalism began in 1964. He spent much of his early career in Tameside and Manchester before moving to Oldham in 1985. His overview of Oldham business is unrivalled. 'Twenty five years ago the new entrepreneurs from Asian businesses were on the outside looking in. They weren't integrated. Now everyone is seen as one. The Asian businesses have made a huge contribution. They employ people; they bring an economic benefit to the town; they are all very ambitious. Not any of them say I'm secure, I want to stay as I am, I'm going to be nice and steady. These guys want to go places. They want to be the next Ajit Medtia, the next Iqbal Ahmed. They see themselves as forging forever upward'.

Is it too early to say?

Assessing the impact of Asian business on the Oldham economy

The newspaper in the photograph reads:

OLDHAM EVENING
Chronicle The One Oldham

FRIDAY, MAY 10, 2013

Finalist: Businessman of the Year

Better by design . . .

create

Is it too early to say?

Assessing the impact of Asian business on the Oldham economy

This book strives to provide an accurate picture of how the Oldham economy has been transformed through the case studies of Asian workers and business people interviewed for the project.

As someone whose career has been closely connected with the Oldham economy both as a participant and observer for the last thirty years of that period I am very aware that it is a personal view. The case studies represent a partial extract, around 20%, taken from the wealth of information contained in the oral history interviews recorded as part of the 'Cotton, Curry and Commerce' project that have been my main source material for this book. These recordings are in the public domain and can be freely accessed at Oldham Local Studies and Archives. They are engaging, entertaining and hugely listenable and I urge anyone whose interest in this period has been heightened by this book to seek out the full recordings.

I can identify three factors in this period that were significant landmarks in the emergence of the Oldham Asian business community which have until the inception of this project not been fully recognised: the expulsion of Indian Asians from Kenya and Uganda; the establishment of Oldham Chamber of Commerce, Training & Enterprise; and the 2001 Oldham riots.

In 1972 about 60,000 Asians, mostly Gujaratis of Indian origin, were expelled from Uganda at 90 days notice. Their wealth and possessions were taken from them and nearly 6,000 businesses along with homes, cars and other household goods were handed over to African Ugandans.

At least half of those expelled came to Britain and several thousand settled in Oldham. Despite arriving penniless and destitute they were skilled and able business people and have since made a great contribution to Oldham's business community. Oldham's gain and Uganda's

loss has to date not been widely acknowledged.

The emergence of Asian businesses occurred 'on the blind-side' of Oldham's business establishment. Oldham Council had responsibility for economic development for much of this period and their concern was with the higher rates of unemployment in the Asian community. They had no strategy for, or awareness of, the contribution of Asian businesses. It was not until the Oldham Chamber of Commerce, Training & Enterprise (OCCTE) was established in 1995 that the potential of Asian businesses was recognised. As a one-stop business support organisation OCCTE had the scale, resources and expertise to help Asian businesses develop and there was a rapid increase in their growth during the OCCTE period.

The Oldham riots of 2001 were perhaps the lowest point in the town's economic history. Yet as is sometimes the case they also marked a defining moment similar to

the 1996 IRA terrorist bomb that destroyed a square mile of Manchester's City Centre. Many in retrospect viewed that event as an opportunity for the regeneration and rebranding of Manchester. Much of Manchester's positive outcome from the explosion was down to the immediate leadership and positive action from the authorities and communities involved.

Unfortunately the same could not be said of the Oldham riots. There was no leader or authority figure stepping forward for Oldham as Mayor Rudy Giuliani did for New York post 9/11. The police chiefs, local authority officers and councillors – perhaps paralysed with shock - were noticeable by their absence during and after the three days of disturbances. It was the business support organisations, Oldham Chamber and Oldham's Asian Business Association, who spoke up for Oldham to the world's media and that were active in the community seeking to reduce tension. It was some days before Deputy Mayor Riaz Ahmad who to his eternal credit took on the mantle of spokesman for Oldham. This was a testing time for the ABA and the wider Asian community and they came through with enhanced reputations and confidence.

So what has been the impact of Asian businesses on the economic history of Oldham? Post-war economic strategy was based around the premise of saving Oldham's cotton industry and part of this strategy involved the recruiting of migrant workers from South East Asia. Clearly this didn't work and by 1980 the town was in a downward spiral of structural decline and economic obsolescence.

Where could Oldham go from here? For a town with such a historic tradition of innovation from the Industrial Revolution onwards the entrepreneurial spark seemed to have died. This project gives clear evidence that it was the entrepreneurial characteristics of the Asian population that enabled the sector to punch above its weight. As Michael Meacher said in his interview, 'they worked hard and sometimes put the indigenous population to shame'.

This was an unintended consequence of decisions taken 50 or 60 years ago by the leaders of Oldham's cotton industry and not as a result of a considered regeneration strategy or deliberate initiative. So had Oldham got lucky? Does this new generation of Asian entrepreneurs give Oldham a level of prosperity better or worse than if the cotton industry had survived?

The history of Asian immigration into Oldham at first sight bears all the hallmarks of the classic model of inward colonisation: low skill and low pay jobs for the pioneer workers; the emergence of embryonic businesses serving the immigrant community; and then business growth via catering, clothing and other cultural consumer products. It is a trail followed by the Victorian Irish navvies leaving a heritage of pubs, music and Celtic culture; the Chinese in the early 20th century with laundries, takeaways, and restaurants; followed by post-World War Two Italians with their rich addition to English cuisine. It is a trail now being followed by the current generation of Polish and Eastern European workers. But it is the sheer scale and impact of the Asian Community on Oldham that completely overshadows the previous immigrant flows and settlements that have fed into the modern Oldham. The change is not complete either. The transformation of Oldham is still underway and the town remains in transition. Is it then possible to make a definitive assessment of how the town has changed – for better or worse?

In 1972 Chinese Premier Chou En Lai's verdict on the effects of the French Revolution of 1789 was 'that it is too early to say'. His answer must hold good for the Oldham question as well. It will be many years of economic assessment before a truly objective verdict can be reached. Another barrier to any fact-based assessment is the lack of accurate business data. From the Industrial Revolution and through the cotton boom years Oldham's economic pulse could be gauged by the number of mills in operation and the total cotton spindleage. After the 1950s no one could say with any certainty how many businesses existed or what Oldham's business wealth was in any one year. Any assessment that can be made must therefore be subjective and rely on estimates and anecdotal and observational evidence. What is in no doubt is that the number of businesses in Oldham increased dramatically during the period of Asian community growth.

In 1982 when unemployment reached a record high of 15,000 people there were perhaps around 2,000 businesses in the Borough. The next ten years to 1992 was the enterprise decade with a huge growth in the number of small businesses and a corresponding rapid decline in larger businesses. Nationally 325,000 businesses in the enterprise decade were started by unemployed people with the help of the £40 a week Enterprise Allowance scheme. Many more started without grant assistance as the national economic landscape changed from a small number of large employers to a huge number of small enterprises. In Oldham, with its base of large traditional manufacturers, small business growth started slowly but then accelerated beyond the national average.

In 1991-2 Oldham Enterprise Agency delivered 884 individual business counselling sessions for 567 new business proposals with more than 400 starting up in business that year. How many of these were from the Asian Community? No exact figures were kept until a survey of Asian businesses in 1997 found there to be about 350 Asian owned businesses. This was out of a total business population of around 2,500 businesses at that time – or about 14% when the Asian percentage of the population was around 10%.

The Government estimate of business numbers, the Interdepartmental Business Register (IDBR), was not made on a consistent basis until 1994 but is probably the best figure available. From 2000 the figure for Oldham went from 2,650 businesses to 3,060 in 2008. This was an increase of 15.5% compared to the 10% North West and England growth rate.

Clearly something was happening in Oldham for business growth to be so healthy over this period. Were Asian businesses the driving force that made the difference?

Given the absence of any robust statistical data analysing Oldham's economic performance there has to be a degree of reliance on the views of people who were part of this era. Though there is complete consistency in the inability of business commentators to back up their views with hard financial statistics, there is equal consistency in their positive views of the contribution of Asian businesses.

'Businesses in 2000 were totally different from when I had left'.

'They had started to develop into new areas, into more mature businesses that could provide employment not just for the family'.

'There are now probably three or four Asian businesses which are now multi-million pound businesses. But there are a lot of businesses that do good business – you don't have to be multi-million pound to be producing a good income and employing people'.

Steve Grant
Business bank manager in Oldham for two spells in late 1980s and again in the early millennium

'There has been a profound change in Oldham consistent with the rise of the Asian community'.

'It is a community that is pretty dynamic, thrusting, ambitious, active and vibrant'.

'Now they are central to the industrial backbone of Oldham'.

Michael Meacher
Member of Parliament in Oldham since 1970

'There is a dynamic business community here, contributing to the local economy and employing large numbers of people'.

Anwar Choudhry
Business adviser in Oldham for eighteen years

'For 14 or 15 years the ABA was a very important part of the Oldham economy. We helped hundreds of small businesses and 15 to 20 large scale businesses.'

Tariq Amin
Chair and now President of the Asian Business Association

'The Asian businesses have made a huge contribution. They employ people, they bring an economic benefit to the town. They are all very ambitious'.

'These guys want to go places. They see themselves as forging forever upward'.

Martyn Torr
Business journalist in Oldham since 1991

Final thoughts

My strongest emotional reaction at the conclusion of the project is one of admiration and respect for those early immigrant workers. How did they have the belief to leave all they knew behind them to travel to a culturally alien, cold and, in many ways, inhospitable Oldham? How did they have the determination to work long hours in jobs deemed too poorly-paid and unpleasant by the local population? Slum conditions, overcrowded housing, baffling language and communication barriers, and a complete absence of religious and social contact outside of work required a certain mental strength to overcome.

Despite being on the lowest rung of the wage scale these workers lived frugally so that they were able to repay travel costs and send substantial funds back to their place of birth to support families left behind. Without recourse to banks and building societies they scraped together enough savings to purchase houses and set up the first Asian businesses. This determination to 'better themselves' was often in the face of hostility of white working class neighbours who did not share these ambitions of betterment.

The early modest businesses were self-contained, sourcing or manufacturing food and clothing to meet the tastes and requirements of Asian culture. The importance of catering and food based businesses, from sourcing spices to providing halal meat, cannot be overstated. It was food-based businesses that spearheaded the break-through to serve a wider multi-cultural and eventually mainstream consumer market.

The subsequent generations of Asian Oldhamers inspire respect and admiration too. The early pioneers, having striven to succeed, put immense pressure on their children born here. An instinctive belief in the importance of education was a 'given' and the children were in no doubt that the huge expectations of their parents had to be fulfilled. In a parallel with the Christian work ethic that underpinned the Industrial Revolution, Asian children had school, attendance at a mosque, and working in a family business to completely occupy their waking hours.

This determination to advance and make a better life was a strong unifying force between all sectors – Indian, Pakistan and Bangladesh – over a period when the home nations were often at war or engaged in uneasy border disputes.

Many of the early generation pioneers comment on how harmonious this bond was in the early days and regret the degree of segregation that has subsequently developed. The emergence of the Asian Business Association as a single entity is testimony to this harmony and the integration of the different Asian nationalities is as much part of their legacy as is the resulting vibrant Asian business community.

Ed Stacey

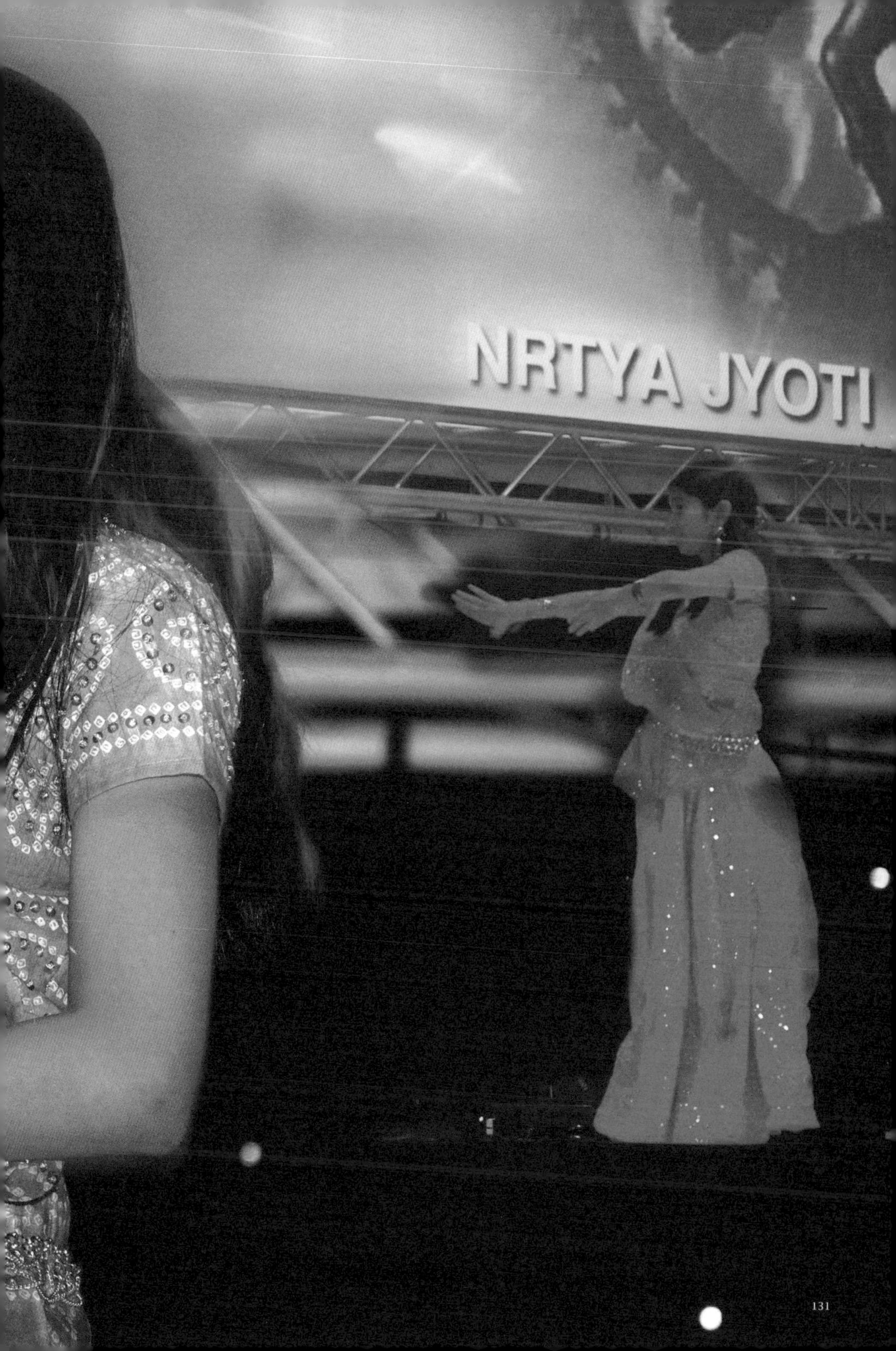
NRTYA JYOTI

Postscript:
Curry Power! The Dil Kush effect on early business growth

History is pockmarked with many milestones other than the dates of famous battles or the reigns of kings and queens. The appearance of new foodstuffs, changes in diet and the development of new cuisines are iconic events often recorded with fastidious accuracy. Europe was importing spice from the Middle East long before the Roman Empire. In the 11th century century Marco Polo brought back cloves, cardamom, cinnamon, star anise, nutmeg, mace and peppercorns from his trips to China and Sir Walter Raleigh introduced potatoes and tobacco from the New World during the reign of Queen Elizabeth the First.

Oldham itself has the distinction of being one of the main contenders for the home of the fried potato when the first chips were fried near Tommyfield Market in 1860. A blue plaque records this event as being part of the origin of today's fast-food industries from which spawned a new manufacturing sector dominated by two Oldham companies. Stott's chip range or Mallinson's frying range became the ovens of choice for most of the UK's fish and chip shops.

The history of Indian food in Britain dates back more than 400 years when merchants of the East India Company brought back a taste for curry from Asia. The first ever UK Indian restaurant is widely accepted to be 'The Hindostani' which opened in London in 1809. Manchester became the fourth city after London, Cambridge and Oxford to host an Indian restaurant when 'The Kohinoor' opened in the 1930s.

It was food - spices and the cooking of curry - that drove the emergence of the first Asian businesses in Oldham. In the early 1960s spices and Asian cuisine were not locally available in Oldham and the only indigenous food remembered with any enthusiasm by the pioneer immigrants was, ironically, fish and chips. However Asian cuisine slowly edged its way into the Oldham palate, at first from delivery vans, and then in the first Asian grocery shops and cafes that in the early days only served the immigrant community.

Eating out in the 1950s and 60s was an extremely intermittent activity usually only occurring on special occasions when the cost could be justified. Oldham was slow to respond when increasing affluence and exposure to different cuisines via the new 'package holidays' boosted the appeal of foreign food in other parts of the UK. It was only in 1955 that the first 'foreign' restaurant, the Chinese 'Lung Wah' opened in the former Volunteer Hotel on George Street in Oldham Town Centre. So when did the first 'Indian' restaurant open in Oldham?

There are a number of contenders for the title of first curry house. The 'Moti Mahal', the 'Light of Bengal' in Union Street, and the 'Noor Jahan' in Featherstall Road have all been in existence since the late 1960s. However the earliest recorded references found so far suggest that the first 'Indian' restaurant in Oldham was 'The Dil Khush' situated at 25 Manchester Street, an area now occupied by Oldham Magistrates Court. The Dil Khush opened in 1961 and was owned by M. Hussain and A. Gapoor.

There is an advert for the Dil Khush from 1967 which suggests that they were targeting English customers as well as Asian families.

A public appeal for information was made as part of the 'Cotton, Curry and Commerce project' seeking information on Oldham's first curry restaurant. The appeal struck a rich vein of nostalgia from members of the public whose first visit to an 'Indian' – though the food was in actual fact Bangladeshi – has remained clear in the memory.

A husband recalls travelling to the Dil Khush from Failsworth to fetch a curry to satisfy the cravings of his pregnant wife and bringing it back in a metal dish given to him by the restaurant – perhaps the first takeaway curry in Oldham? Others remember enjoying cheap lunches at the Dil Khush when attending the 'Oldham Tech[74]' in the 1960s.

A local resident whose father spoke Urdu remembers his dad helping translate official forms for the restaurant staff. Another diner, a teenager at the time, was treated by her uncle to her first ever outing to a restaurant. Her uncle didn't care for curry and ordered steak. She remembers how exotic it was to be in an Indian restaurant! However the building was old and situated in a redevelopment area; a visitor to the Dil Khush recalls a pipe bursting on an upper floor and drenching the diners below! The building was finally demolished in the 1970s to enable the building of the current Magistrates Courts and M. Hussain, one of the proprietors of the Dil Khush opened a new restaurant called 'The Priory' on nearby Manchester Road.

The importance of these early 'curry' businesses cannot be overstated. From these extremely modest beginnings has grown the thriving takeaway, restaurant and catering industry of the present century which is a major employer not just in Oldham but across the UK. Indian food has become Britain's favourite cuisine with the then Foreign Secretary Robin Cook famously proclaiming in 1980 that chicken tikka masala was the true British national dish.

Many manufacturing, wholesaling and distribution businesses have thrived in Oldham supplying the curry and catering sectors. Two outstanding examples of international multi-million pound businesses are Amin Poultry and the Seamark Group both of whom started from corner shops in Oldham in the 1960s.

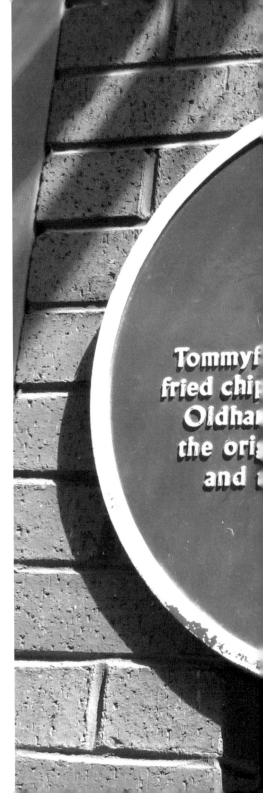

SAPERE · AUDE

SH AND CHIPS

d, home of the first British
The first chips were fried in
round 1860 from which
s of Fish and Chip shops
"Fast Food" industries
can be traced.

Appendix:
Appendix of Business Organisations and Directors

Asian Business Association Limited
The ABA operated as a membership division of Oldham Chamber from about 1996 until 16th June 2003 when the ABA incorporated as a limited company. ABA Ltd then worked in partnership with the Chamber in the Chamber's various organisational structures until about 2010. The members and directors then resolved that as Asian businesses were now part of the mainstream business community it's work was done. ABA Ltd was dissolved on 27th December 2011. The directors who served in ABA Ltd were: **Kurshid Ahmed; Daood Akram; Tariq Amin; Shafaat Chaudhry; Anwar-ul-haq Choudhry; Gita Chudasama; Gunvantsingh Kumpavant; Angela Mahandru; Arshad Mahmood; Fiaz Mohammed; Ramesh Mohandas; Mohammmed Rahiem; Mohammed Shahid; Bharatkumar Sisodia; Akhtar Zahid.**

Chamber of Commerce history
Oldham Chamber of Commerce has had four distinct limited company structures over a 121 year history: Oldham Chamber of Commerce from 1882 to 1919; Oldham and District Incorporated Chamber of Commerce from 1919 to 1995; Oldham Chamber of Commerce, Training & Enterprise (OCCTE) from 1995 to 2001; and finally back to Oldham Chamber of Commerce from 2001 to 2003 when it was merged into the Greater Manchester Chamber of Commerce.

Oldham Chamber of Commerce has its origins in a meeting called by the Mayor of Oldham on 23rd November 1882 where a decision was made to form a Chamber of Commerce which met for the first time in February 1883 with 147 members at Oldham Town Hall. The Chamber has a proud history of action on behalf of Oldham's industries with successful campaigns for a reduction in railway charges, the construction of the Manchester Ship Canal, the provision of telephones, improvements to Oldham's road systems, and the growth of cotton in the British Empire rather than the United States. It was as a direct result of the Oldham Chamber of Commerce's actions on this last point that the British Cotton Growing Association was founded.

The Chamber's first registered office was Oldham Town Hall where it held its meetings. In 1919, to reflect its widening geographical base, the Chamber became Oldham and District Incorporated Chamber of Commerce. When Oldham Town Hall closed the registered office moved to offices shared with their accountants D. R. Harrison & Co in Clydesdale Street.

The decline in the cotton industry had a large impact on the Chamber. In 1890, 111 of its members had been cotton-spinning firms. A century later there were only ten. By the beginning of 1992 total membership stood at just 170 and the Chamber moved to new premises at the Meridian Centre, Ashton Road. In October 1995 it was announced that Oldham Chamber of Commerce, Oldham Enterprise Agency, Chamber of Trade and other business support bodies would merge with Oldham Training and Enterprise Council to form the Oldham Chamber of Commerce, Training and Enterprise (OCCTE). OCCTE was the only chamber in the country to have a Business Link as an integral division rather than a separate company. Other divisions within the Chamber included the Asian Business Association and Oldham Export Club. Membership of OCCTE reached over 1000 businesses in the late 1990s, the highest by percentage of business population in the UK.

However in 2001 changes in Government funding for workforce training forced a de-merger and a scaled-down Oldham Chamber of Commerce relocated to Oldham Business Centre, Cromwell Street. In 2003 further business service funding changes necessitated a widespread merger of chambers throughout the UK and Oldham, together with Manchester & Tameside, Bolton & Bury, Wigan, Rochdale, Trafford, Salford and Stockport chambers, merged to form the Greater Manchester Chamber of Commerce (GMCC) with offices in Oxford Street, Manchester. Oldham businesses are represented within the GMCC by Oldham Chamber Council, a division of the main chamber comprised of elected business members.

Boards of Directors for Oldham Enterprise Agency, Oldham Training and Enterprise Council, Oldham Chamber of Commerce, Training and Enterprise and Oldham Chamber of Commerce

Oldham Enterprise Agency was formed in 1985, merged into Oldham Chamber of Commerce, Training & Enterprise in 1995 and the company was formally dissolved in 1997. The directors who served were: **Craig Pickering, David Bellis, Richard Fenby, Janet Larton, Paul Vincent, Terry Largan, Jack Hartley, Ken Hickson, Ian Torr, Richard Curry, David Read, Riaz Ahmad, Keith Coates, Councillor Bernard Judge, Kay Coleman, Colin Greenfield** and **Ed Stacey.**

Oldham Training and Enterprise Council (Oldham TEC) was formed in 1989. In 1995 the name was changed as various business support agencies merged into the Oldham Chamber of Commerce, Training & Enterprise. The directors who served were: **Norman Stoller, Rodney Greenwood, John Hall, Paul Roberts, Neil Mckay, Khurshid Ahmed, Gloria Oates, Roger Hinchliffe, Councillor Jim Greenwood, Philip Lees, Councillor James McCardle, Councillor John Johnson, Frank Hodgkiss, Tariq Amin, Ruth Paisley, Philip Marsland, Craig Pickering, David Bellis, Richard Fenby, Jack Hartley, Ian Stott, Richard Curry, Riaz Ahmad, Keith Coates, Councillor Brian Mather, Kay Coleman, John Gracie, Mark Lewis, Shafaat Chaudhry, Peter Dowbakin, Eric Williamson, Bob Smalley, Geoffrey Pugh, James Troop, Anthony Lewis, Ian Howarth, Dr Fred Aughton, Patrick Newstead, Keith Antrobus, Sabiha Shahzad, Councillor Margaret Riley, Councillor David Jones, Phill Brown, Reg Chapman, John Whiteside, Dr Bill Kneen, Robin Henshaw, George Gatley, Peter Maybury, Michael Mealing, George White, Edmund Gartside, Peter Shrigley,** and **Peter Mount.**

Oldham Chamber of Commerce was founded on 14th March 2001 and closed in 2003 when it merged into the Greater Manchester Chamber of Commerce. The company was dissolved in 2005. The directors who served were: **Rodney Greenwood**, John Hall, Eddie Dixon, Pauline Pawlykiwskji, Paul Roberts, Neil Mckay, Khurshid Ahmed, Gloria Oates, Roger Hinchliffe, Ed Stacey, Councillor Jim Greenwood, Philip Lees, Councillor James McCardle, Councillor John Johnson, Frank Hodgkiss, Tariq Amin, Raymond Glynne-Owen, Ruth Paisley and **Philip Marsland.**

Endnotes

1   *Coincidentally Elk Mill was the last mill to spin cotton in Oldham when it closed after some seventy years of spinning in 1998*

2   *A temporary but short lived rebound*

3   *The site was re-developed some 10 years later for a supermarket, housing and canal marina*

4   *By their first name*

5   *To arrange his marriage*

6   *The bus driver*

7   *Vans*

8   *When I started out*

9   *That had been saved to buy a tractor*

10   *The two countries*

11   *Air mail letter*

12   *Without the letter*

13   *Kashif Ashraf*

14   *Tariq Amin of Amin Poultry*

15   *For the Asian Business Association*

16   *Anwar Choudhary*

17   *The school was a two site school at this time*

18   *At North Chadderton School*

19   *This became Malbro Group of Companies*

20   *A £3 million development part funded by a £1.3 million Millennium Commission grant*

21   *Central Mosque*

22   *Bangladeshi Association*

23   *Play truant*

24   *Working in a clothes shop in Manchester*

25   *A project supported by DCMS and EHRC*

26   *For construction sites, local authorities, warehouses*

27   *Boxer*

28   *Former President of Pakistan*

29   *Cricketer and politician*

30   *Boxer*

31   *Footballer*

32   *Snooker professional*

33   *The ABA*

34   *1968*

35   *Ramsingh*

36   *In the North West*

37   *Named after Ramsingh's daughter born in 1971*
38   *2001*
39   *The ABA Board*
40   *The company now processes 150,000 birds a week*
41   *Jagatsingh*
42   *In Gujarat*
43   *Indian*
44   *In 1970-1972*
45   *In Oldham*
46   *ZAN has now become Openwork Ltd*
47   *Henna designs to celebrate the forthcoming wedding*
48   *At the Cash & Carry*
49   *In 2004*
50   *Temporary skin decorations for festivals and ceremonies*
51   *In the town centre*
52   *ABA*
53   *In Glodwick, Oldham*
54   *Mashukul's father*
55   *For financial help*
56   *Early 1970s*
57   *Failsworth*
58   *From his early days in the UK*
59   *Food hygiene*
60   *In electronics in 1984*
61   *Through fashion magazines*
62   *With the Careers Service*
63   *Asian Businesses*
64   *In the Industrial Revolution and cotton industry boom*
65   *Business correspondent for 30 years*
66   *Income level*
67   *Motorways*
68   *On the Saturday*
69   *2001 was a general election year*
70   *1988*
71   *In Oldham*
72   *Of the ABA in 1998*
73   *Engaging with ethnic minority businesses*
74   *The name by which Oldham College was known*

List of Illustrations

We would like to give thanks to all who have contributed images to this publication and for their kind permission to reproduce them.

Photographs copyright of Oldham Council can be obtained from Oldham Local Studies and Archives, **archives@oldham.gov.uk**

Photographs copyright Realtime Images can be obtained from:
lesh@realtimeimages.co.uk

Photographs copyright of The Oldham Evening Chronicle can be obtained from:
Oldham Chronicle, 172 Union Street, Oldham, England OL1 1EQ

Photographs copyright of New Image can be obtained from:
Studio@newimage.co.uk

Photographs copyright of Jahans Photography can be obtained from:
info@jahansphotography.co.uk

P16-17
Asia Mill, Clayton Street, 1982. Ref: P8125. Copyright: Oldham Council.

P19
Firs Mill, Failsworth, looking towards Oldham, c.1930. Ref: P14201. Copyright: Oldham Council.

P22
Holebottom Colliery, Fairbottom Street, c.1870. Ref: P20564. Copyright: Oldham Council.

P25
Cotton Spinning, c.1920. Ref: P20701. Copyright: Oldham Council.

P26-27
Elk Mill, 1929. Ref: P14313. Copyright: Oldham Council.

P29
Raja Mohammed Mushtaq Ahmed, c.2012. Copyright: Mushtaq Ahmed.

P30-31
Wellington Mill, Greenfield, 1976. Ref: P7301. Copyright: Oldham Council.

P33
Akhtar Zahid, 2013. Image by: Jahans Photography. Copyright: Oldham Council.

P34
Akhtar Zahid at Vitafoam, 1968. Copyright: Akhtar Zahid.

P35
Akhtar Zahid working for SELNEC buses, 1970. Copyright: Akhtar Zahid
SELNEC bus, 1970. Copyright: Akhtar Zahid.

P36-37
Ring spinning machinery, c.1960. Ref: P9681. Copyright: Oldham Council.

P38-39
Waterloo Street, Glodwick, 1977. Ref: P511. Copyright: Oldham Council.

P40
Mohammed Ashraf, 2013. Image by: Jahans Photography. Copyright: Oldham Council.

P42
Abdul Malik, 2013. Image by: Jahans Photography. Copyright: Oldham Council.

P44
Abdul Mannan, 2013. Image by: Jahans Photography. Copyright: Oldham Council.

P47
Mohammed Rahiem, 2013. Image by: Jahans Photography. Copyright: Oldham Council.

P49
PS Events Limited, c.2010. Copyright: PS Events Limited.

P51
Ramsingh Kumpavat, 2013. Copyright: Realtime Images.
Gunvant Kumpavat, 2013. Image by: Jahans Photography. Copyright: Oldham Council.

P52-53
Mina Stores, Ashton Road, Oldham, c.1980s. Copyright: Kumpavat family.

P54-55
Opening of the Indian Association Temple, Schofield Street, Hathershaw, 10 July 1999.
Copyright: Kumpavat family.

P56-57
Corner of Waterloo Street and Bismark Street, Glodwick, 1975. Ref: P5605.
Copyright: Oldham Council.

P58-59
Civic Centre, Oldham, c. 1977. Ref: P47985. Copyright: Oldham Council.

P60
Arshad Mahmood, 2013. Image by: Jahans Photography. Copyright: Oldham Council.

P63
Tariq Amin, 2013. Image by: Jahans Photography. Copyright: Oldham Council.

P65
Amin Poultry trucks, Featherstall Road, 1996. Copyright: Tariq Amin.

P67
Bharat Sisodia, 2013. Image by: Jahans Photography. Copyright: Oldham Council.

P69
Indian Association Community Centre and Shree Radha Krishna temple, Schofield Street, 2013. Copyright: Oldham Council.

P71
Medtia Place, Union Street, 2013. Copyright: Oldham Council.

P72-73
Anisha Ali, Floral Heaven, Copsterhill Road, 2013. Copyright: Realtime Images.

P75
Gita Chudasama, 2013. Image by: Jahans Photography. Copyright: Oldham Council.

P76
Nazia Saleem, 2013. Image by: Jahans Photography. Copyright: Oldham Council.

P79
Shurjahan Begum, 2013. Copyright: Jahans Photography.

P80-81
Sabeen Ashraf and client, Revival Beauty, 2013. Copyright: Jahans Photography.

P82-83
ABA Business Awards, 2008. Ref: M166/9/7/19. Copyright: Oldham Council.

P84
Wasim Aslam, 2013. Image by: Jahans Photography. Copyright: Oldham Council.

P87
Mashukul Hoque, 2013. Copyright: Mashukul Hoque.

P90-91
ABA Business Awards, 2008. Copyright: Realtime Images.

P93
ABA Food hygiene training, c.2002. Ref: M166/17/7. Copyright: Oldham Council.

P94
Anwar Choudhry, 2002. Copyright: Anwar Choudhry.

P96
Kashif Ashraf, 2013. Copyright: Kashif Ashraf.

P99
Abdul Malik and Tariq Amin, ABA Awards, 2008. Copyright: Realtime Images.

P100
Greenhill Store, Glodwick, 2013. Copyright: Realtime Images.

P103
Ajit Medtia, c.2006. Copyright: The Oldham Chronicle.

P105
Iqbal Ahmed, c.2001. Copyright: The Oldham Chronicle.

P106-107
The Oldham Business Centre, 2004. Ref: 39772. Copyright: Oldham Council.

P109
Launch of the ABA, 1998. Copyright: The Oldham Chronicle

P110-111
Desi Sweets and Treats, Union Street, Oldham, 2013. Copyright: Realtime Images.

P113
Michael Meacher, MP, 2013. Copyright: Michael Meacher.

P115
Steve Grant, 2013. Copyright: Steve Grant.

P117
John Gracie, 2013. Copyright: John Gracie.

P119
Martyn Torr, c.2013. Copyright: Martyn Torr.

P120-121
Dsgn UK finalists in two categories at the Oldham One Business Awards, 2013. Copyright: New Image.

P123
Oldham Town Centre, 2013. Copyright: Oldham Council.

P130-131
Nrtya Joyti Dance Troupe, ABA Awards, 2008. Copyright: Realtime Images.

P133
Blue Tiffin Restaurant, 2013. Copyright: Realtime Images.

P134-135
Blue plaque, Tommy Field Market, Oldham, 2013. Copyright: Ed Stacey.

P149
Ed Stacey, 2013. Copyright: Ed Stacey.

Sources

Primary Sources
Oldham Advertiser newspapers and archives
Oldham Chronicle newspapers and archives
Oldham Local Studies and Archives:
- Asian Business Association archives (Ref: M166)
- Oldham Chamber of Commerce archives (Ref: ABJ)
- Oral history recordings from 'Cotton, Curry & Commerce' project (Ref: M185)

Secondary Sources
Home Office & Bedfordshire Police Authority: Business as Usual (section on the 1996 Manchester bomb)
Brian R. Law, 'Oldham Brave Oldham: An illustrated history of Oldham'
Mary B. Rose (ed), 'The Lancashire Cotton Industry – A history since 1700'
Migration Policy Institute: 'Building a British model of integration'
Oldham Economic Review Spring 2012

Other Sources
Companies House and Duedil: Company Directorships
Wikipedia and internet search engines
Working papers and documents held by the author

About the author Ed Stacey

Ed Stacey was born in London in 1949 and obtained a BA in Public Administration at Sheffield Polytechnic and then business adviser qualifications at Durham University Business School. He then worked in marketing and economic development for Corby New Town, Leicester, Sunderland and Washington New Town before moving to Oldham in 1985.

In Oldham he has headed the Oldham Economic Development Unit, Oldham Enterprise Agency, Business Link Oldham and Oldham Chamber of Commerce. From 2003 he has worked as a business consultant, a freelance business and property journalist for the Guardian Media Group, and lectured part time in business planning for the University of Huddersfield.

He lives in Saddleworth in a self-built eco-house with Lyn his wife and has two adult children. In addition to writing he currently runs a tourism business with his wife and is chair of the Co-operative Group North Manchester Area Committee.